A Handful of Quietness

A Handful of Quietness

HAROLD ROGERS

WORD BOOKS, *Publisher*
Waco, Texas

Library of Congress catalog card number: 77-075463
ISBN 0-8499-0010-7
Printed in the United States of America

For Rae
who since our college days
has weathered the storms
and shared the calms with me

Contents

Preface

There it was! A handful of quietness.

Like many who venture into the open, I always hoped to eventually stumble over a rock or piece of flotsam and beneath it discover a prize of intrinsic worth. Then one day I found it, not on a surf-pounded reef or at the edge of a glacier, but tucked away in the Bible among pages not often turned: "Better is a handful of quietness than two hands full of toil and a striving after wind" (Eccles. 4:6).

I read and reread those words, turning them over with the fingers of my mind, but like a rock encrusted with age they needed long and careful polishing before their true value was revealed.

A handful of quietness . . . was there any place for it
in a world of hurry and worry?

And so I argued with myself . . . for a monk in a
cloistered cell . . . a lonely shepherd in an alpine meadow
perhaps, but for those on life's teeter-totter, when? where?
Yet the idea of quietness, the silences, would not go away.
I knew the possibilities were unlimited, but when? how?

While I continued to make newspaper and magazine
deadlines and crisscross the country to keep speaking engagements, I began to read the contemplatives: Thomas
Kelly, Thomas Merton, Evelyn Underhill, Brother Lawrence, Thomas à Kempis, St. John of the Cross, the Cloud
of Unknowing, and of course the Bible, especially the
psalms. Elton Trueblood and Thomas S. Kepler helped me
greatly.

Little by little, as I viewed these persons and other out-
standing Christians, I began to sense that the life of the
Christian should be like an iceberg. The bulk of it is hidden
deep within the fastness of Christ while that which is
visible to the world sparkles with the beauty of calmness
and peace. This, of course, means living on two levels, with
the interchange from one to the other not visible to the
onlooker but real to the participant. It means automatically
bringing all concerns and involvements into the presence
of God, seeing them in the light of his love and purpose,
and responding to them with love and confidence. Rather
than being an escape from life, moments of quietness serve
as a preparation for life as God would have us live it, but
the direction of life is fixed at the hidden level. This does
not always mean a physical retreat to a closet. Rather, while
we are discussing and planning in a busy atmosphere, we
are quietly tuning in for a clearer image of the divine
presence.

That there is an overall governing purpose, a controlling
force, few of us doubt, but in our dash to get, to go, and

to be, our goals become so diffused that we fail to concentrate on the true center—God as exemplified by Jesus Christ and his guiding presence in our lives. We give momentary lip service to the idea when we should be cooperating with it; as a result we have become *thing* conscious rather than God conscious.

Looking at my own life and at the lives of my contemporaries, I am reminded of Thoreau's idea that we live lives of quiet desperation. Often in the evening, while reviewing the day's activities, I repeat the words of Wordsworth's sonnet:

> The world is too much with us; late and soon,
> Getting and spending, we lay waste our powers:
> Little we see in Nature that is ours;
> We have given our hearts away, a sordid boon!

And so I began experimenting. I still am for that matter. Before writing these words I have had many times of quietness and have taken long, solitary walks. Today I watched a cardinal high in a hackberry tree, listened to the age-old melody pour from his throat, and in that moment felt a confidence and knew whom I could trust.

For those who would experiment as I have and am, my suggestion is, don't shout to attract God's attention; be still and recognize his presence, power, wisdom, and love. In true meditation the only voice to be heard is God speaking to us, not our speaking to him. The answer to any of our problems is to have union with him and then to give him complete cooperation so that he can work his will through us.

We do not scourge ourselves with guilt because we are not disciplined to long intervals of contemplation; rather we thank him for those few snatched moments of quietness we do share together, and we look expectantly to more moments in an apprenticeship of love.

Preface

This title is honest. A handful of quietness is so little, but the benefits derived from these moments will be so wonderful that before long they will become a natural part of life. Then there will be a regular time so nicely fitted into a busy schedule we will wonder why we have been so long in arranging it, for we will discover that quietness is the basis for achievement.

1. Rough Water

The desperate cry of the psalmist, "Save me, O God! For the waters have come up to my neck" (Ps. 69:1), has been echoed across the centuries by countless thousands who felt they were about to be swept away by the torrents of life. A seemingly impossible task has just been assigned by one in authority. An accident or critical illness has occurred. A financial disaster looms. Marital discord is wrecking the home. Loneliness is overwhelming.

Not all crises are of this magnitude; lesser upsets can shatter one's complacency too. The woman driving a hookup for the neighborhood children suddenly discovers the battery of her car is dead. A man compiling the family income tax returns cannot find some needed information.

Guests are coming for dinner, and the oven unit burns out, or the family dog digs up the neighbor's garden. These events can assume overwhelming proportions. Like rubber bands, nerves stretch to the limit and threaten to snap.

This is the time to think of the presence within, for our lives are centered in that presence. While the branches of a tree may be tossed about, even broken in a storm, the tree will survive if the roots hold fast. Meeting daily routine without losing the sense of God's presence may require a lifetime of practice. Mental habits of inward orientation must be repeated over and over like any other good habit until they become automatic. True, there will be lapses and failures, real discouragement; yet even the least attempt in this direction will bring its rewards. This was the secret of strength and self-control for the early followers of the Way, the practice of keeping the presence uppermost in their minds and looking to the joys ahead.

As a canoeist, I long ago learned that after running rough water there is usually a quiet pool where one may pause and say, "We made it." Just the thought of this is often enough to sustain and calm in time of turmoil. The psalmist, who upon occasion cried out in despair, also said, "He leads me beside still waters" (Ps. 23:2).

Perhaps there are as many solutions for handling the rough waters of life as there are persons and situations: Have a temper tantrum, panic, suffer a nervous collapse, cry out desperately as did the psalmist. Yet there is another way: Pause at the moment of impact and picture, not the rough water to be run, but the most peaceful scene one can imagine—the pool beyond the rapids.

For me there is a clump of white birch growing on the shores of a northern lake. Years ago, in the evening hours when the long shadows of the land had stretched out over the water, I would drift along in a boat, sometimes casting slowly for bass but mostly just looking and listening. The scene is so etched in my memory that even in a crowded airport when schedules have become fouled or in a newspaper office with deadlines looming and news breaking fast I have paused to relive that moment, quieting the confusion that was jamming my mind, then moving ahead.

A woman tells how years ago, on the farm where she was reared, there was a tree-shaded spring. It bubbled from beneath a canopy of rocks, formed a small pool bordered with blue violets, then trickled down to a crystal clear brook. Often when she wished to be by herself, she would go to that spring, drink from its water, and sit quietly, watching the cloud shadows play over the land. She says it is more than a quarter-century since she has been to that spring; still in moments of stress she mentally returns to it, drinks of its water, sits on the hillside, and regains her composure.

A professional man in a demanding position keeps a picture on his office wall. It is a country scene with a dirt road bordering a humble farm home. When demands become so great he scarcely knows which way to turn, he will take a moment to look at that picture. Mentally he begins at one horizon and walks along the road past the farm home until he comes to the other horizon. He says that he can smell the dust, feel the breeze on his face, and hear the creak of the old windmill; in those moments he relaxes in mind and body.

In moments of stress many of us want to return to places where there are memories of peace and security. In John's Gospel (10:40) we read that when Jesus was harrassed and threatened he went back across the Jordan where he had been baptized, perhaps to recall that here God had said he was a son with whom he was well pleased.

To escape even by forming a mental picture takes our minds off ourselves, our fears, our confusions, and opens us to a state of receptivity in which the presence of God can be made manifest and help us to reorganize our thinking. Quietness is the bridge across which one may travel to bring his or her life into harmony with God's intended purpose. It is the more direct approach. Plunging into a chasm of bewilderment, even despair, then slowly struggling up the far side, slipping and falling, expends energy which might have been conserved by using the bridge of quietness. It is not an escape from the strange but a way to recognize the familiar. It thus becomes a form of adventure for which the only equipment necessary is spiritual.

We get quiet, not just to get quiet, but because tension, anger, and fear block out common sense. Our job is to get quiet and remember who we are, children of the most high. We find the answer to what is troubling us by letting God do his perfect work in and through us.

He knows, and we know, that we are not just one person but a whole committee of persons, each striving for center stage—breadwinner, parent, homemaker, social participant, and so on. That the majority of us have too many irons in the fire, there is little doubt, but having cast our lot we are forced to live with it until we are able to reassign ourselves in order of life's priorities. In that snatched moment of quietness, in the middle of routine, we pause and affirm that we are children of God and that he is able to help us handle the details as an all-wise Father if we will but afford him the opportunity.

Faith in God never depends on faith in something or someone else. We have faith in him first, and then we arrive at faith in his power. If God is in control, there is no need to feel insecure. Things may happen which suggest insecurity, but this does not mean there will be insecurity. It probably means that a personal plan has been blocked, perhaps only temporarily. There is a divine plan. A person sees only with human eyes, but the divine plan is for all of life, for all the universe. A loving Father will never plunge us into rough water and abandon us. He is there, loving, protecting, strengthening, regardless of the outcome.

An eminent pastor said to a man facing bitter disappointment, "Just when you think God has forgotten, he shows up."

We get quiet. We turn to him even momentarily, not to a God who is far off, but to his presence inside us. Jesus said, "The kingdom of God is within you" (Luke 17:21, KJV). The kingdom of God—the rule of God, the love of God, the power and wisdom of God—is right in the midst of us, in the center of our being. It is wherever he rules the hearts and minds of people. There are two sets of laws: the laws of natural man, and the laws of God's kingdom which supersede the laws of man. While we do not ignore the laws of man, we depend more on the laws of God.

In that brief interval of quietness when by mental effort we transport ourselves from the moment of confusion to peace and calmness, we can say as did the Apostle Paul, "Now to him who by the power at work within us is able to do far more abundantly than all that we ask or think" (Eph. 3:20). In that instant we are no longer alone.

Quietness by itself is never adequate any more than science by itself or even a religious belief is enough. In union with God we find strength and completeness. When we are centered in him, he is our life. We are a part of his reality.

While we cannot stop our thinking, we can to some extent control our thoughts. We can clear our minds of the clutter that is beginning to take over—fear, worry, hate, resentment, and other disturbing thoughts—and open ourselves to receive God's good, power, presence, and direction. If God is a life-creating, life-sustaining force, is he not also a life-changing force? We may be the most lonely, frustrated, frightened person in the world, but the God who works within us can change all that if we will be quiet and give him our "wills" rather than our "won'ts." This means complete trust in him. However, such trust seldom comes all at once. It comes through trial and error, through experience. It is learning and knowing that God will help. It is like learning to swim. We cannot learn to swim until we trust the water to hold us up, to support our weight. We may flounder and splash until exhausted and still sink. That is why the beginner is taught the dead man's float, simply stretching at length face down on the water and letting the water furnish total support without any effort on the swimmer's part. Once a swimmer has learned to trust the water, the most difficult strokes can be mastered. We begin by trusting God a few moments at a time. Just because there is not a sudden flashing of lights or a great moment of ecstasy does not mean his presence is not with us. More often than not he is only a still, small voice, speaking so softly that in our rush we fail to listen.

A woman tells how her husband was critically injured in an automobile accident. She says that when the call came and an emergency vehicle rushed her to the hospital where they had taken her husband she knew he was dead. In those moments she asked God for strength and suddenly realized she was acting calmly, that she was able to make decisions, call the family and tell them of the accident.

In the days of adjustment and loneliness she came to realize that God had been with her throughout her entire life. His presence, even those times when she had not realized it, had sustained and guided her through illness, rearing a family, and now in the loss of her mate.

Complete trust dispels panic. It leaves one free to act and provides clarity of mind. When we are calm, our faculties are sharpened. We say that a person keeps his or her cool. That is what trust enables one to do. The one who keeps cool passes the examination, works through a crisis, and faces criticism or impending danger and is victorious.

When we become agitated about our surroundings, our families, our friends, or our fellow workers, we are unable to be much help in finding right answers. Our tension blanks out the power of the presence within us. Left to our own devices we lash out in all directions.

It is difficult to imagine a person performing a demanding task while paralyzed with fear or committing a loving deed while harboring revenge and hatred in the heart. It is impossible to work efficiently while burdened with resentment because of the assignment or toward the one making the assignment.

There is an acid test for our faith: Deep down inside, in the midnight of our being, can we live in quietness and confidence and find strength for the rigors of life? A vital, life-sustaining faith must be more than a creed about God. It must be a personal experience with God that is so intimate we trust him with every detail and move forward with complete assurance that he is entirely dependable as our guide.

Quietness, calmness, trust, and union with God are not only for the crisis situation but for any time, all the time, anywhere, and for everyone.

Repeatedly the question is asked, Where do I begin? My days are already filled to the brim, and you suggest I take time for a period of quietness. When? The questioner becomes uptight, threatened by the mere suggestion of one more demand.

Regardless of the circumstances, I know of no better time to begin than right now, right where you are. A moment of quietness, no matter how brief, can bring a new perspective that can be felt and that can serve as an influence throughout the hours ahead. There is both a calming and a claiming spirit. As soon as we start something with a nervous burst, we are called back by the admonition, "Be quiet! Trust God!" This is the time to pray with the psalmist, "Let the words of my mouth and the meditation of my heart be acceptable in thy sight, O Lord, my rock and my redeemer" (Ps. 19:14).

Throughout the day, in our quiet moments, we will think about those words and make them our guide. We will repeat them over and over again. We will measure our thoughts and actions by them.

Whatever the circumstances, if the words we speak and the thoughts we think are acceptable to God, there is little to fear. If one does not need to be ashamed of the inner life before God and if one is truthful, there is no need to cover tracks. The one who speaks no evil of another can face everyone without hesitation and live with an openness which in itself brings peace. We become careful of our actions and reactions. We think before we speak. We take control of our thoughts, channeling them to him. When we link ourselves with him, our thoughts become positive rather than negative. Our actions reflect our God-nature rather than our selfish nature. When we practice turning to him, day by day with cooperative attention, a new kind of strength is born. Where there is true cooperation with God, there is not fear but complete, loving trust.

True, demands are still present. The problems have not all vanished, but the approach has become different. In that moment of quietness there was a transaction from the way of self to the way of God. It is not a time when we seek to change God's attitude toward us; rather we are changing our attitude toward him and toward others, for in true meditation we would know nothing but his will for us. To live in God's presence even for a moment is to have a patience and a serenity that nothing can touch. Times of quietness are not waiting and hoping; they are times of commitment, a willingness to carry out God's directives. In so doing we find strength and peace.

The *Upper Room* once ran the story of two artists who agreed to portray the idea of peace. One painted a beautiful mountain lake. Its waters were quiet and undisturbed. There were no clouds in the sky. All was serenely beautiful. The other artist painted a thundering waterfall with a twisted tree growing out over the tumbling water. Just above the reach of the spray was a nest, and in it a mother bird was feeding her young. In the judgment of the spectators, the second carried the higher conception of peace.

Perhaps that is what most of us seek in this hurly-burly world, not escape, but peace that comes through trust.

Just as we are advised to pray without ceasing, we aim unceasingly toward quietness in the inner life. Of course, at times we will forget and become upset, but in the brief prayer, "Let the words of my mouth . . . ," we have a target toward which to lift our sights. In the conference room, in the marketplace, on the highway, at home, we snatch moments to think of those words and of him to whom they are directed.

Because we have become such activists, we tend to think in terms of the outer life of service and to ignore the inner life, that oneness with God. This is like trying to raise plants without roots. Before Christ calls us to a cause, he calls us to himself. This does not mean neglecting the outer life of service but strengthening it with the inner life of devotion. Remember: Christ withdrew from the multitudes, even from his disciples, to be alone with God, but he always went back to serve.

Oh, I know too well the arguments. This is all very well for one who has plenty of time—the monk, the hermit, one who has retired from active life—but for the person on the treadmill where every step causes it to run faster and faster, when?

Odd moments! Yes. A dozen or a hundred times each day. Added together they amount to a good bit, but should there not be a more disciplined time? If so, when?

Most definitely there should be a time, the length of which will be determined by circumstances and by the one observing the period of quietness. Gerhard Groote, the Carthusian monk who lived in the fourteenth century, wrote: "If you will withdraw yourself from the useless talk and idle goings-about, as well as from novelties and gossips, you will find leisure enough and suitable for meditation."

Dr. Paul Tournier, the Swiss psychiatrist, has written in *The Person Reborn:* "If the first quarter of an hour of the working day were devoted to meditation in common, the productivity of the work instead of going down would increase."

Yet to neglect using the odd moments as a time to realize our oneness with God is to neglect some of the best opportunities to enrich life, to work more effectively, and to find purpose and happiness rather than discouragement and drudgery.

For the early morning riser, there is no better time than before the day's activities begin, and there is much to be said for using this time to practice the presence of God. Take a few moments to think about him, become receptive to his direction, and thank him for the sleep that has been enjoyed. For one who feels under pressure in the morning, a few moments may be enough, with snatched intervals throughout the day, until there is a more suitable time.

Personally I prefer the evening just before retiring. I like to walk out under the stars or turn out the lights, go to the window, and look up at the sky for a few moments, then settle down to an unhurried time of quietness. I read the

Bible or some other spiritual book, listen to choice records, or just sit quietly and meditate. But whatever the time, I do not let it become a period of bondage. If I feel edgy and cannot comfortably get quiet, I find some external activity.

However, resting in silence is not merely lazy-hazy drifting. If there are prayer requests, this is the time to make them known, not with fervent pleading that leaves one more uptight than before, but with quiet confidence that a loving God will answer in his way and time. We do not try to persuade God to do our will but to persuade ourselves that he knows better than we do and then to accept it. Quietness and prayer are never a means of evading responsibilities. We often try to use God rather than let him use us. Certain things can only be done by us or by God working through us. These we cannot escape.

In moments of silence we also become aware of who we are and that like all persons we are a dual creation. We are mainly conscious of the outer self, and we tend to spend most of our efforts in satisfying it. But there is also an inner person, that oneness with God which is the true self and which may be found if we desire and are willing to discipline ourself in that direction. Only when we accept this inner self and bring the outer self into harmony with it do we find peace and purpose. We find a power to walk on higher ground and to identify with him, which is our ultimate goal. This is not an attainment reserved for a select few; it is a way for all who wish to follow it and who, without reservation, will accept the opportunities available.

When we are thoroughly involved in the outer life, as we are during most waking hours, it may be difficult to remember the truth about ourselves. In the time of quietness we move from the world of appearances to the world of reality. We offer ourselves to God so that he may do with us what he has been wanting to do but we have prevented because of busyness and insistence on following our desires. At this time we make self the first offering, giving body, mind, and spirit to him without reservation for his high and holy purpose. This, perhaps, is the most important feature of quiet time.

This is also a time to ask that we be made aware of any wrongdoing, of any imperfections in our lives that need correcting, and it is the time when we firmly resolve to do our part in making the necessary corrections.

However, moments of quietness, whether in the morning, at midday, or in the evening, are not hard-fast methods or formulas. They are times to develop an attitude of faith, openness, attention, reverence, expectation, and above all joy that we can come into the presence of the Father. It is like that intimate time a child spends with his or her father. Often words are not necessary; it is enough just being together.

In his Western novel *The Burning Hills*, Louis L'Armour paints a graphic word picture: "She said nothing; she thought nothing. She was at this moment an Indian, at one with her world."

In that bit of description we see a person completely quiet and relaxed, almost blending into the landscape. To bring it into our particular focus, we might say, "She said nothing; she thought nothing. She was at this moment a child of God, at one with her Father."

A time of quietness, to enter into the silences, is to find those moments when one is unaware of all external forces and aware only of union with God. At such times we are not only quiet; we are confident that he is at work, directing us toward our highest good. It is a time of reverent, dedicated listening for the voice of God.

2. The Little Foxes

"Wait a minute!" Perhaps that phrase has caused as much irritation as any three words in our language.

A friend, whose wife has the habit of always asking him to wait, laughingly tells how he placed the Bible in a convenient spot and during the first month they were married read the entire book of Genesis while waiting for her.

"Hurry up to stand in line to wait" is a frequent remark made by military personnel.

All of us spend time waiting—waiting for someone who is late for an appointment, waiting for a bus or plane, waiting for a repairman, waiting for a telephone call or letter, waiting for someone to make a decision, waiting in a doctor's or dentist's office. Few of us wait with any degree of patience unless it is while we are fishing. Even there the old method of sitting quietly with a cane pole and cork bobbing on the surface of the water while we contemplate the antics of a water-strider has given way to casting or trolling with the motor running so we can cover more territory in less time.

Moment by moment, while we wait, our impatience grows. Every nerve in our bodies becomes taut. If we allow them to, these times of impatience can become "the little foxes, that spoil the vineyards" (Song of Sol. 2:15).

Rather than letting times of frustration cause us to say an unkind word or plunge us into a hasty action that will turn the day into shambles, let's use these moments to become quiet and turn our thoughts to God. We can release our cares to him constantly with thanksgiving that he will take them and draw us even closer to him.

Recently I watched a blind man waiting for a traffic signal to change. He stood quietly, leaning on his white cane. His head was cocked a bit so that his ears could better catch the sounds of traffic that he might be able to judge when its direction changed. Two persons who had their sight stepped off the curb. One leaped back to avoid being struck by a car hurrying to beat the change. The other darted in and out and finally made it across the street. The blind man quietly waited. I looked at his face. It was composed, trusting.

When the signal changed I said, "Now we can go."

He replied, "Thank you. It's a beautiful day, isn't it?"

I prayed, "Lord, forgive me. He never sees a sunset or a sunrise, yet he can say, 'It's a beautiful day.' "

Now when I am tempted to become impatient, I picture him standing quietly, and I say to myself, "It's a beautiful day."

Those who achieve, who are happy, and who are able to cope with life are poised, self-controlled, and confident.

They are fun to be with, dependable in times of emergency, and naturally do more with less effort. However, poise is not the exclusive property of a select few. Anyone can acquire it with a bit of discipline that comes with the desire and determination to control tension which seems to surface at the slightest provocation.

No person need be ashamed of honest emotion—sorrow, indignation, love, happiness; even these may be muted to our advantage. What we are concerned with here is the snappishness and the irritation that some unexpected interruption or delay causes.

Perhaps one cause for irritation is an exaggerated sense of self-importance. We should not look upon ourselves as either holier or better because of a particular position or degree of attainment or because of the unusual way we live. God sees us all as his children, though different in certain respects. Surely he has been patient with us.

Another cause of impatience is the feeling of inferiority, self-depreciation, quite the opposite of the first but no less difficult to handle. (If I were so and so, you can just bet they wouldn't keep me waiting.) If we are important to God, and we are, then we are important to self—too important to let irritation spoil our day.

We may be trying to be someone we are not. The fear of being found out makes us jittery, quick to look for little things, to go on the defensive and allow anger to come to the front.

Argument—how often we hear an opinion expressed contrary to ours, and we launch into a heated verbal exchange that does little or no good toward finding a solution. Instead it builds barriers, creates tension, and ruins poise. To state a different point of view quietly and without antagonism is entirely different from heated argument.

Being set in our ways, unwilling to change, to modify our schedules or views for the sake of another and for peace and harmony, is another cause of mounting impatience and friction. No one honestly wants to be called "hard-headed as a mule."

However, an irritant causing impatience may be our own fault. By all means remove it rather than wear it like a hair shirt. I once knew a man who bought an expensive pair of shoes that did not fit. His attitude: I'll wear them if they kill me. Not only did they hurt him, they hurt his family, his employees, and his friends until they would have much preferred him to go barefoot.

Patience is necessary, for many disturbing things occur daily. However much I may try to be at peace, my days cannot be without some annoyance. The unexpected continually interferes with my schedule. Some annoyances are my fault; others are not. I may be hurrying to finish a manuscript and at the end of a page discover I have left out a very important sentence. I start again, and the telephone rings. This is the time to slack off, to go to the window for a few minutes and do a bit of sky watching.

Just outside my window I see a cardinal sitting impatiently in the locust tree, waiting for a purple grackle to finish eating at the bird feeder so he may come and take his turn. Sparrows will come and eat on the opposite side of the feeder from the grackle, but not the cardinal. Of course, sparrows will eat anywhere, but I watch Mr. Cardinal. I am not sure what keeps him away. It could be fear, but the sparrows are much smaller and they eat with aplomb even though the grackle is only inches away. Again it could be that the cardinal is jealous. He has beautiful red feathers and such a nice topknot, but perhaps he would like shiny, purplish-black feathers. But whatever the cause I say to myself, "Now the sparrows are adaptable, they adjust to the circumstances and are enjoying a good meal.

Apparently the cardinal cannot or will not. . . . Can I adjust, or do I stand at a distance and impatiently wait?"

In *A Journey with the Saints*, Thomas S. Kepler has written: "The secret of the revolution in the lives of the saints lies in the fact that their lives are centered in God. They never seem hurried, they have a large leisure, they trouble little about their influence; they refer the smallest things to God—they live in God."

For years I kept a copy of that statement on my desk at the office. Often while waiting for the telephone I would read and meditate, not only about those words, but about God and my relationship with him. Those little nudges are necessary to cause me to pause and think.

When we become quiet and center our lives in God, we begin to see how much time is frittered away by detail, how much we need to simplify so that we will have time for him, for others, and for ourselves. It is not being selfish to plan a few moments alone with self.

Hurry and worry are worse than the ten plagues of Egypt. Recently I visited a friend in the hospital. Someone had sent him a cartoon. On it was the picture of a doctor examining a man's chest with a stethoscope, and the doctor was saying, "All I can get is a busy signal."

My friend said, "This is the best thing that ever happened to me. For the first time in my life I have been quiet so that I can really think."

We spread ourselves too thin. Untold numbers of men and women are obsessed with the idea that the really good part of life is to keep busy. In our constant hurry we have no time to come quietly into Christ's presence and sit at his feet. We often strive toward perishable goals, toward unnecessary enterprises. In St. Luke's Gospel (10:38–41) we read about the Master's visit to the home of Mary and

Martha. One can almost hear the person addicted to busyness say, "But without Martha the work would never have been done." Still Jesus said Mary chose the better way.

However, for some, even while meditating on the Marys and Marthas, there will be the specter of the clock. Civilization has caused us to become clock watchers. "You're going to be late for school . . . The bus will be here in five minutes . . . My appointment is for three o'clock sharp . . . I promised to meet her at seven-thirty." Even the most phlegmatic person is haunted by the clock.

That is why I prefer late evening for my prolonged time of quietness. I think of Meister Eckhart's statement: "Time gone a thousand years ago is now as present and as near to God as this very instant." I reaffirm that I am glad God has all eternity to work out his purpose and is not limited by man's clock.

In times of quietness there should be at least a few moments when time stands still. When the secret place of our being is turned into a constant-demand center rather than a sanctuary of trust and obedience where we know all things are ours because they are Christ's and we are his, we are trading our birthright for a mess of potage.

Prayer, trust, and quietness are never an evasion of responsibilities. If we listen in the true spirit and with honest commitment, we are simply placing ourselves in readiness to obey any command our Lord may give, knowing that with the command comes the necessary power and wisdom.

There are two verses in the Bible I have tried to make mine, but too often impatience has taken over. "Commit your way to the Lord; trust in him, and he will act" (Ps. 37:5). "Trust in the Lord with all your heart, and do not rely on your own insight. In all your ways acknowledge him, and he will make straight your paths" (Prov. 3:5–6). Much heartache could be avoided if we would truly commit our desires to him and let him act in his own good time. Many false starts would never be made if we waited for him. That he has an overall plan for every life I have no doubt; yet in our impatience we plunge ahead without listening. We say we must act now or the opportunity will be lost.

I was once quite unexpectedly offered a new position. I thought it was in a location where we would very much like to live. The opportunity, the salary, everything about it seemed much better than where I was. Without hesitation I accepted. That evening, when I got quiet, I asked God about it. There was no answer, and I took it for the go-ahead signal. But early the next morning I awakened suddenly from a sound sleep. Everything in me was saying, "Don't change! Don't change!" I could scarcely believe it, but the conviction persisted; so I notified my intended employer I could not accept his offer. A few months later I had an opportunity to be with him. He had found another person far more suitable for the task than I would have been, and I had grown increasingly happier where I was. It would have been a decided mistake for all concerned had I gone.

How ill advised some of our snap judgments are. It is when we look to God and fix our will strongly in his that he is able to act, perhaps not at the very moment we desire, but he sees our course to the end of life's journey; we see it only to the next curve in the road.

Many times others have come to me with the complaint, "I'm in a dead-end job." And many of them have been correct. Surely no one knows how many people are unhappy in their occupations. One cannot blame them for desiring a change. They dread waking up to a new day. Now there is nothing wrong with change if it is the right change. To such persons I can only say, "Beware that you do not forget God's purpose for you. Think carefully. Get quiet.

Give God time. He can only do *for* you what he can do *with* you. As long as you are bitter, angry, impatient, you are short-circuiting him. Keep yourself open, be responsive, accomplish what needs to be done now."

Abraham Lincoln is credited with saying, "We will only be as happy as we make up our minds to be."

Every day is God's gift. We need to grab hold of it and hang on to each precious moment. There is no need to put off happiness, thinking that with change we will find it. We might be happier, but every day can become perfect when we try to communicate our love and understanding to all with whom we come in contact.

When we trust God with patience, we will make the right decision. When we pray and have faith, he can act. Faith is never standing still. It is holding fast and becoming creative. God reveals his plan for us through his Word, ideas, and circumstances, but these do not always bounce up like popcorn. When one's mind is centered on a problem, and on the problem alone, creative ideas are obstructed. God is the great revealer of ideas. Our task is to be open to them. In the words of a golfing friend, "Hang loose and follow through."

We waste much of life with hurry and impatience. We fail to see the good things about our present situation while we are waiting for the better. We may be in the very place God wants us even though we cannot see any results in what we are doing. A golden opportunity may be only hours away if we are open to it.

More than once I have stood under a giant oak and, holding an acorn in my hand, have asked, How long does it take an acorn to grow into a sturdy tree?

Many great things in life are accomplished by a slow growth process rather than by a sudden overnight blooming.

However, if one is dissatisfied with his or her present

situation, the very spirit of God could be bringing about the sense of dissatisfaction. Perhaps this is the inner voice saying, "You are ready for other things. Look about. Make preparation. And when the time comes, move with courage to the new challenge."

Today many are beginning to realize this restlessness, this inner longing, cannot be satisfied with material things, and they are earnestly seeking ways of greater fulfillment and service. They are seeking with a truly unselfish spirit to make their lives more meaningful to God and to their fellow men.

A word of warning: If there is doubt about any decision, wait until God opens or closes the door so there is no mistake. He will do it in his own good way and time without turmoil and disappointment. To act on impulse is to invite difficulties that may take years to remedy.

Not only do we pray about the situation, but we check our impulses and our desires with his Word. Two men were about to enter a business partnership. One was a deep, spiritually motivated man, the other was not. All other things considered, it seemed like an ideal arrangement, but the man who trusted in prayer and the Bible turned again and again to these words: "Do not be mismated with unbelievers. For what partnership have righteousness and iniquity? Or what fellowship has light with darkness?" (2 Cor. 6:14). The partnership was never consummated. A year later the man who had turned away from what seemed like a golden opportunity said, "It would have been the mistake of my life."

Still we are prone to argue, "Everything in me says . . ." The spirit, the true inner presence, is never contrary to God's holy Word. He guided the Children of Israel with the cloud by day and the pillar of fire by night. Today we have the Scriptures as our dependable guide.

Our society is tuned to excite every nerve, every desire in our being, to keep us at the highest pitch, to tempt us to the limit and create new desires and passions so that we may be swayed in a particular direction. When these tensions and desires become paramount, we forget God's spirit lives in each of us. He cares for us and is working in us. Therefore, if we are alert to his leadings, we must also put him first in our desires. We become still and know that he is God.

In every realm of life there is a correct answer. Sometimes we fail to see it because we are so concerned with our decisions and with all the other tugs and pulls demanding our attention. Our freedom, our opportunity, comes from accepting the mind and thoughts of our Lord for us. He does not regard us as objects. We are children of the most high, the one who is all wisdom, love, and power; so we have no need of fears or impatience if we trust him to direct us, to give us courage and common sense to follow his leading.

Definitely, there will be times when the path ahead seems unmarked. Even to take a single step seems fraught with danger. This is the time to pray, "Open my eyes that I may see . . ." It may be that the direction will be for us to wait with patience. We may be directed to take a single step. Seldom is the whole journey revealed; yet we find the way by reading his Word, listening to his Word, and living his Word. We can be sure that God will never lead us too fast or abandon us. When he says, "Wait a minute," it is we who become impatient and let go of his hand only to plunge into deep water. His will is ever for our good, but he must have our complete attention and obedience.

A good teacher would never attempt to explain a problem in higher mathematics or philosophy while there was confusion or inattention on the part of the learner. How then can we expect the Creator of the universe to impart great truths to us, guidance and direction, while we are overly concerned with our self-importance and desires?

John Woolman, a devout Quaker who lived in the eighteenth century, is a good example. He might have become wealthy at his trade of tailoring, but as his business increased and he found it absorbing more and more of his thoughts, he began sending customers elsewhere. He determined to arrange his worldly affairs so as to be attentive every moment to the voice of his Lord. Nothing else held a place of greater importance than his attentiveness to the voice. He simplified his way of living so that he might ever move closer to the real center of life.

When we are quiet, attentive, and undisturbed by outer desires and influences, we see and hear beyond the ordinary. Such are the moments of greatest creativity, courage, and happiness. They can and do change lives. We have all said, "I didn't know what the next move was going to be when an idea came to me . . ."

The big question is, Do I have the courage and perseverance to do God's will when it is clear to me?

The fountain of Christian life has its origin in that quiet place where there is only God and I. This is the source of our inspiration and where the great decisions of life are made. Nothing we ever do will get the all-clear signal unless it is first received in this quiet center. All thoughts, actions, and habits are formulated here. Our lives are shaped by the thoughts we think, by the gods we choose. What are they? Prestige, power, popularity, prosperity? Our Lord said, "But seek first his kingdom and his righteousness, and all these things shall be yours as well" (Matt. 6:33).

What does all this have to do with patience? True patience comes as a result of trust in a wisdom higher than our own. When we trust, we act rather than react. Often it is our reactions that cause the trouble. In our anger, frustration, fear, and passions we react impulsively. We say and do things that moments or years later we may regret.

Sometimes this anger and frustration are directed at God himself. Only the other day a woman said, "I cry out to a God who is nowhere around."

Many are burdened because they have prayed about a condition, perhaps health for themselves or a loved one, and seemingly nothing has happened; there has been no response. Yet we cannot know how much progress has been made because of that prayer. Often we do not see the results we visualize, but they are there.

No prayer, no centering in God, is ever wasted. No prayer is without results if it has been prayed with any semblance of faith. Growing and change are part of every prayer and every life. Change is living. We may walk through difficult experiences, but always the presence of God is there to sustain, change and heal. We may not understand, but as we come to accept his presence in every fiber of our being or with the one for whom we pray, a confidence is born that overcomes all barriers. There comes a peace and trust, and tensions slack as we remember that the complete will of God is always good. We may stand in the way of it by unconsciously thinking, "There is only one way, my way. I will accept no other."

This is why we need times of quietness. Quietness is not pure rest and relaxation. It may be that, but it is also more: It is becoming aware of God's presence in our lives and being willing to carry out his directives. This may involve struggle and doubt, for sometimes the period of quietness becomes a battlefield—the outer against the inner. But little by little as we talk it over with him, even to the most minute detail, if we are open and willing, a moment comes when we need no longer hurry and worry. All we have to do is live that moment so all our life reflects the image of Christ. Then he will take care of tomorrow. In fact, he probably has a better plan for tomorrow than we can make if we go after it hammer and tongs. Many times the best thing we can do is keep hands off tomorrow. We have business enough for today. With that thought in mind we relax and know that the only thing of importance is to live for God and in God. We accept his promise at full value: "Turn to me and be saved" (Isa. 45:22).

3. Magnetic North

We awakened on a small island in Lake Agnes in the Canadian wilderness and were completely walled in by fog. Only the high-pitched, quavering cry of the loons which echoed and reechoed from behind that white curtain broke the stillness.

When I left the tent and walked down to the water's edge, it was all backwards. I knew we had approached the island from the southeast the night before and had beached our canoes on a ledge of rock on the eastern shore, but during the night the island seemed to have turned completely around. I looked skyward for some evidence of the sun, but there was only a ghostly whiteness. North, south, east, and west were all the same. There was just the spot where I stood—cold, damp, and lonely—and the hiss of little waves curling at my feet.

I took a compass from my pocket, placed it on the trunk of a fallen pine, and waited for the fluttering needle to settle down. In a matter of moments, the needle was pointing, not where I thought it should, but in an entirely different direction. I picked the compass up, shook it, and replaced it on the log. Again it pointed in the same direction.

Everything in me said, "It's wrong! It has to be. Perhaps there is some mineral in the area attracting it."

I felt doubt as I seldom have. Still time after time I had been warned by guides never to doubt my compass. Follow it always, they had insisted. Years of experience had proven this advice sound. A few hours later when the fog burned away, the island swung back into position, the compass was accurate, and we knew the direction we should follow for the next leg of our journey.

As we paddled across the lake, I remembered a few years earlier when three of us had been caught in one of those sudden blizzards high in the Black Hills of South Dakota. Because we were familiar with that section of the hills, we had neglected to carry a compass, a careless oversight. Night came on quickly, and somewhere in that tangle of peaks, canyons, and whirling snow we made a wrong turn. Hours later, exhausted, cold, and considerably chagrined, we saw the light of home and realized our mistake.

I always recall those two occasions when I meditate on these words of Jesus: "I am the way, and the truth, and the life; no one comes to the Father, but by me" (John 14:6). Just as the compass points to magnetic north, Jesus points the way to the Father. We may try other ways, but we discover there is only one true way. We stumble around without his direction.

I often begin my quiet time by trying to picture Jesus

and by thinking of some things he said and did. I feel his presence though not his form. He reveals himself to me without showing his face; yet because he becomes very real, it helps me to know God. The only description we have of God was given by Jesus, "He who has seen me has seen the Father" (John 14:9).

If we are to love, to realize, to obey, and to follow willingly and trustingly, we must personalize. It is difficult to love or trust an abstract. When we personalize by visualization, Jesus, the divine Son of God, becomes real to us; as a result, the Father becomes equally real and approachable. Our thoughts of an impersonal God, a great force, or a God of might and anger vanish, and in their place we have a God we can know and love.

It is easy to become sentimental over Jesus at Christmas time—a baby in a manger with his parents, the shepherds and wise men bending over him. But he grew up and became a man. He was tempted even as we are by the material and by prestige and power. He, a person even as we are, resisted the most tempting offers, and by his every action he shows us the way.

As we become quiet, as we listen and feel, something still greater—his irresistible love and sacrifice—reaches down into our innermost being and tugs at our heart strings just as that invisible force swung the compass needle in the direction of magnetic north.

Never do I go to a military cemetery and look at the rows and rows of white markers but what I think here lie those who were willing to die that I might live in freedom. I never hear of a peace officer being killed in the line of duty but what I think he gave his life that I might be safe either awake or asleep. Just as those persons gave their lives in line of duty, our Lord gave his life in a duty of love and obedience that we might have life now and forever.

At another time Jesus said, "I came that they may have life and have it abundantly" (John 10:10).

We may question what he meant by that. Definitely not material or prestige or power. He did not rule those out if they are obtained in the proper manner and used in the right way, but his teachings are for something far greater than anything which may be so easily lost. He came that we might have one to love, to trust, to be with us in all life, to give direction so that we might live on a higher level than mere existence with nothing but darkness at the end.

Wherever the teachings of Jesus have been made known and followed, the life-style has been upgraded. There has been progress and more freedom. Until we turn from self to him, we will never know true freedom from hate, envy, frustration, and insecurity. All these may be exchanged for love and trust.

Experiment. Try his way for thirty days; honestly try it. Rather than merely thinking about his way or even learning about it, we make it our way. We center our life in his until we can truthfully say, "It is no longer I who live, but Christ who lives in me; and the life I now live in the flesh I live by faith in the Son of God" (Gal. 2:20).

I also picture Jesus walking along the shores of Galilee. There he saw some unwashed fishermen and was willing to number them among his most trusted friends. They were ordinary men until they met the Master and followed him. If they could become what they did with his help, what about you and me?

Isn't it wonderful to know that he did not go just to those in places of high position but also had time for the lost and the least?

I remember talking with a black shoeshine man in a Southern state when racial tension was high. I asked if he were ever afraid. He replied, "The Lord is my shepherd. That's all I need."

During off moments I find myself thinking about other things Jesus said, "I am the light of the world" (John 8:12).

My thoughts turn back to that morning on the island or the night in the blizzard. It's easy to get lost when there is no light. Still he is always waiting to welcome us back; in fact, he will come to meet us if we give any evidence of returning to him.

I see his tremendous sense of forgiveness and justice when he stooped down and wrote in the sand while the woman taken in adultery stood before the mob, trembling and in fear for her life. Jesus imposed no harsh penalties, made no accusations, and issued no calls for an explanation; he extended loving forgiveness and gave a simple directive, "Go and sin no more."

Again I see Jesus at prayer, slipping away early in the morning while others slept or taking time after an exhausting day of teaching and healing to be alone with God. I see him in those last agonizing hours in the garden with the cross looming closer and closer. Even there his great prayer was for others—God first, others second, self last. I believe in prayer. I pray because Jesus prayed and taught us how to pray.

Suddenly I hear his ringing call for service, "If any man would come after me, let him deny [forget] himself and take up his cross and follow me. For whoever would save his life will lose it, and whoever loses his life for my sake will find it" (Matt. 16:24–25).

Forget self! But self is all we have. If we forget that . . . Forgetting self and surrendering the will has nothing to do with emotion; it is true action—yes or no. The Lord will never force himself into our lives. The choice is ours. We may shift like a weather vane with every new idea, or we may lock ourself into his will, but we determine our action, no one else.

And so we begin to serve others, to give a cup of cold water in his name, to visit the sick and those in prison, to hold out a helping hand to the downtrodden. By so doing, even though we may lose the life we had planned, we shall find another, one even more thrilling and more rewarding than our greatest dreams.

Still this is not the end of the story. Much as I am drawn to Jesus in all these instances, I am drawn even more to him as I picture him after the resurrection. I see him with those courageous women. I hear him say, "Go tell Peter . . ." Go tell the one who denied me at the most critical time that I am coming back, not to get him or to seek revenge, but because I still trust him to carry on my work.

I see him walking into the sunset along a dusty road with two bewildered men headed toward Emmaus, taking time to explain to them all the wonderful things that had happened.

Later he was so patient with Thomas, helping him overcome his doubts.

I see him at the seashore in the early dawn, building a fire, preparing breakfast for some of his disciples who had returned to their trade following the crucifixion and had fished all night.

At times his words, "I am the resurrection and the life" (John 11:25), hold meaning in the fullest sense of the word. Life now. Life forever. O grave, where is your victory?

Down the corridors of time I hear the voice of the Roman captain, whose men had carried out the execution, say, "Truly this man was the Son of God!" (Mark 15:39).

Finally, after everyone had had his say, our Lord said, "I am the Alpha and the Omega, the first and the last, the beginning and the end" (Rev. 22:12). Kings and kingdoms may pass away, but he will still be the same—unlimited by time or space.

Suddenly I am faced with the startling realization: I will only know as much about him as I dare practice in my daily life. The master teacher said, "If you have ears, listen! And be sure to put into practice what you hear" (Mark 4:23–24, LB).

Listen, listen, listen. The Holy Bible, his Word, is speaking to us if we will but listen and accept the challenge. To make his teachings and his example part of our lives means to take a path that leads into light and life. It is more than a mere creed or a code of ethics; it is reality. It means using our God-given potential to the utmost.

4. Blisters

The Dakota sun was spilling out of a cloudless August sky when I clambered down into the canyon and over a jumble of rocks. A pint-sized man in a floppy hat and cracked boots was loading a wheelbarrow with dirt to push down to a rocker by the creek.

"Howdy," he said.

When I returned his greeting, he cupped his hands over the shovel handle and put his whiskered chin on his knuckles. "Rest a spell." He indicated a box that obviously had once held dynamite. "Water in the crick is cold if you're thirsty."

I thanked him and availed myself of both the water and the box. "Finding any color?" I asked.

He shrugged. "Not much. I can just about make wages, but it's here. Question is, Can a man find it? I've been prospecting better than forty years now."

"Not many of your kind left," I said.

"Nope," he said. "Lots of 'em try, but soon as they come up with a bunch of blisters, they mighty soon lose interest."

I think of that old prospector every time I pick up J. Cameron Peddie's little book *The Forgotten Talent.* Peddie tells that when he felt he might be getting a call to the healing ministry he set aside the hour from eleven until midnight every night when he did nothing but wait quietly for some direction. Three, four years passed. Then in the fifth year, not in his time of quietness but while he was peeling potatoes at the kitchen sink, he was given the signal for which he had been waiting.

One full hour of waiting quietly every night for nearly five years . . . forty years of prospecting . . . soon as they come up with a bunch of blisters, they mighty soon lose interest. What a picture to contemplate for those of us not quite willing to go all out in our quest for oneness with God.

We are activists. We look for sensory satisfaction and become easily bored. When something does not happen immediately, if we do not give up entirely, we continue in half-hearted fashion. We forget the way of the cross is not always easy.

Often we use times of quietness and prayer to try to convince God to want what we want. We see him in our perspective rather than seeing ourselves in his perspective. Few of us like the word *surrender* when the surrender of our every wish to him should become the most important part of our quiet time. Until we are entirely his, to do with as he pleases, he can do very little with us or for us.

However, surrender does not automatically and instantly guarantee desired results. Always we are expecting some sensory response. We want to hear, to feel, something. We want it as definite as the pointing needle on a compass. We want all our problems to disappear now. As a result, we spend too much time pleading with God to make certain directions clear to us, even trying to make deals with him, rather than quietly praising him and reverencing his presence living within us.

The prophet Isaiah said, "O Lord, thou art my God; I will exalt thee, I will praise thy name; for thou hast done wonderful things" (Isa. 25:1).

The psalmist sang, "I will sing to the Lord as long as I live; I will sing praise to my God while I have being. May my meditation be pleasing to him, for I rejoice in the Lord" (Ps. 104:33-34).

A time of quietness is first a time of praise and affirmation; in that light we voice our requests without specifying the "how." In simple childlike faith we leave the procedures entirely up to God. I so much like the scriptural description of Abraham: "No distrust made him waver concerning the promise of God, but he grew strong in his faith as he gave glory to God, fully convinced that God was able to do what he had promised" (Rom. 4:20-21).

For longer than I can remember I have prayed. Prayer has always had some part in my life, and yet I would feel quite safe in saying that 98 percent of my prayers have been asking prayers, either on my own behalf or for someone close to me. Many times they have not only been asking prayers, but they have been frantic prayers, uttered in a tense moment of need or indecision. Unfortunately, rather than waiting for direction, I have plunged ahead, taking things into my own hands as if I had never prayed at all, only to find myself in an even greater dilemma.

In a vague sort of way I knew that one finds life by trusting God, but to be perfectly honest I wanted life on my own terms. While I wanted God's love, protection, and even his help, I did not want the restraints and obligations this relationship might impose. Like a child living in a comfortable, well-provisioned home, I wanted security along with the right to go my own way with the privilege of returning if I made a mistake. Battered and bruised I might return to it for help, but while I was well and felt capable, I asked just how much God would change my plans if I capitulated. After all, I had goals, desires, hopes. I was willing to work and sacrifice to attain them. I made the motions; all I wanted was his second.

For example, I wanted to be one of the name outdoor writers in America, and I wanted God to aid me in those plans. I asked for his help. I implored. I offered a few deals. And I did write regularly for one of the larger outdoor magazines, even became a member of the editorial staff, but a day came when that door was closed and locked tight. Looking back, I do not believe there was anything basically wrong with my desire. What I did not know then was that apparently there were other plans for me, more-fulfilling plans which would lead to greater adventure and would use my outdoor background as a real steppingstone.

Because of my avid love for the out-of-doors, I have spent many hours in the forests, in the mountains, and on lakes and rivers, hours of solitude and contentment. For long intervals I have sat quietly, not really thinking of anything, just absorbing the sights, the sounds, and the smells of the wilderness around me. Today, living in an apartment in a large Southern metropolitan area, these experiences are as real as when they actually occurred, and so I draw on them just as I am doing now.

I call upon my memory to see trees silhouetted against the sky, shadows cast by mountain peaks, the crash of the surf. Imagination becomes a true helper as I relax in moments of quietness, as do pictures, beautiful music, a poem.

At one time a beautiful little mountain stream meant much to me. It was a retreat from the frustrations of the world. Often I would go there and sit on a rock, watching the shifting shadows of the pine and aspen as they played on the rippling waters. In those moments I sensed a presence I could not see or touch but could feel.

I shall never forget those moments on the edge of that mountain stream, for it was during the depths of the Great Depression. The salary I received as a public school teacher was not adequate to support a young and growing family. There never was a day when I did not pray desperately for a better job. I wrote scores of letters, but without results. And so I would go down to that little stream to lick my wounds and pray more desperate prayers.

I felt that if I continued to bombard God with my asking prayers, there was a chance my persistence would pay off. I remembered the widow before the judge (Luke 18:1–8). It seemed that because of her persistence she was finally granted her request. I wanted my requests granted in like manner. I did not realize then that perhaps while she waited she had changed so the judge could grant her request. We often pray for a new job, a better job, when in reality we are not ready for it. There may still be lessons to be learned right where we are if only we would settle down and learn them, perhaps patience and trust if nothing else.

Deep within we feel that if we pray long enough, promise enough, and place ourselves in the proper position we will receive that for which we pray. We tend to forget that God, like any good father, should often refuse a request for the child's own good.

Recently a father bowed to his teenage son's demands for a motorcycle. Two days later while the boy was in the emergency room at the hospital, following an accident when he had plunged off the highway at a high rate of speed, the father lamented, "Why didn't I say no?"

One day, in a prayer retreat, it hit me square between the eyes. A man stood up and asked, "Who are we to tell God? Are we his equal when it comes to making decisions? If we are, why don't we quit praying and go ahead with our own plans rather than involve him at all? What we need to do is get quiet and recognize God for what he is —omnipresent, omnipotent, and omniscient.

In true prayer—in our times of quietness—we listen expectantly for God's direction, love, and orders, knowing he is everywhere, all power, all knowledge. If there is some condition or decision causing concern and we do not know which path to take, our part is to turn to God and let him direct our efforts. Through faith we pray that our minds will be directed and that we will take the right course of action even if it is only to wait.

It is easy to repeat "For the Lord gives wisdom; from his mouth come knowledge and understanding" (Prov. 2:6) only to forget and take things in our own hands.

We avoid false starts and poor decisions by praying for wisdom and good judgment, knowing that God is far more ready to give than we are to receive. When the thought pattern comes, we then follow it even though it be different from what we had first hoped.

However, if we have acted hastily, if we feel we have made the wrong turn, the thing to do is get quiet and ask God to forgive us for our hurry and put us aright. Often we spend needed time in regret, thinking, "If only I hadn't done this or that." We need to stop looking back and let God correct us and direct us, even to learning from our mistakes.

The psalmist wrote from experience, "The steps of a man are from the Lord, and he establishes him in whose

way he delights; though he fall, he shall not be cast head-
long, for the Lord is the stay of his hand" (Ps. 37:23–24).

We often wait too long to seek direction. We wait until
disaster strikes, and God is not as easily found in chaos as
he is in quietness. While God is there, because he is everywhere, we who are praying and seeking are so tense that
it is almost impossible for him to get through to us. Many
people who have been lost in the forest or mountains and
have died from exhaustion and exposure after running
around in circles would have been saved had they only
stopped and waited for rescue.

In a real sense this has become autobiographical. To the
charges of slothfulness and impatience in my spiritual exercises, my times of quietness, I would have to plead guilty.
As I have been writing these words, I am reminded of the
admonition in Luke's Gospel, "Physician, heal yourself"
(Luke 4:23).

There have been more times of failure and discouragement than I care to remember. In those times of waiting,
when nothing seemed to happen and my mind wandered
or I fell asleep, I remembered the words of the old prospector, "Soon as they come up with a bunch of blisters,
they mighty soon lose interest."

If only we could realize the great good that comes from
true meditation. Here a whole new realm is discovered—
the presence of the living God. During these moments the
life that becomes completely obedient, shutting out all
voices but the one, finds an astonishing completeness. The
Master was thinking about such a time when he said,
"When your eye is sound [your whole purpose single],
your whole body is full of light" (Luke 11:34).

During these times we may sense a full understanding of
God's will, love, and mercy and realize our complete dependence upon him. However, this must be more than

theory. It must translate into our life and into the lives of others when we make self totally available to our Lord. Then he will find a place for us, but this takes patience; our times of meditation will take us through many dry and barren places. We look to those who have found this true center of commitment and living for inspiration and steadfastness. We would draw strength and courage from their example.

When the day or night comes that during my time of quietness I can say with truthfulness, "For God alone my soul waits in silence" (Ps. 62:1), then will I know that I have taken my own medicine.

But before that happens there must be discipline. All worthwhile accomplishments require discipline. Moving into our times of quietness we say, "I am closing my mind to all but the words of God as he would have me hear them."

At this point many are prone to say, "But God no longer speaks to us as he did to the prophets of old."

In a measure perhaps such an argument is correct, but God does still speak to us. We have the Scriptures. We also have a great host of witnesses for example. We have that quiet inner voice, not a human voice, yet a voice that communicates if we listen with expectancy and willingness. Perhaps he speaks far more than we realize, more than we want to hear, for true hearing demands obedience.

Our job is to listen and obey and to teach our body and mind to relax until there is no longer struggle. His way is our way.

5. A Snail's Pace

An elderly man who had lived by the Book, as he said, tells of meeting a stranger who had just participated in a nonstop Bible-reading marathon. Selected persons had taken turns reading aloud, day and night, until the entire Bible had been completed. The stranger asked if the elderly man knew the Bible.

"Not as well as I might wish," was the reply.

It developed that the stranger had been one of the readers. "Most of it was pretty dull going," he remarked. "Oh, there were a few interesting spots, but they were quickly covered."

The one who had spent his life with the Bible suggested that next time they take at least a year for their reading.

The stranger smiled with amusement. "There are too many other things to read."

Yet the elderly man knew the way to become acquainted with the Bible is not in a race against the clock but in reading it slowly, listening, enjoying, and then living the words that for him and his family had become a roadmap of life. Often he would quote the psalmist: "Thy word is a lamp to my feet and a light to my path" (Ps. 119:105).

If you wish to profit from reading the Bible, the most productive speed is a snail's pace. A great portion of time will be spent in thinking, absorbing, picturing, applying, and asking, What do these words say to me today as I plan my course of action? A verse or two at a time may be enough. For one who reads in this way, the goal is not how long it takes, but how can I learn to walk closer with God?

There is a strange fascination in reading the Bible in this manner, for the journey, no matter how many times taken, is forever revealing something new—a word, a thought, a direction. One time a thought will be passed over lightly; the next it will be filled with significance. It is like standing on a mountain peak and looking out across the valley; the vistas are ever changing. There is always something new, something different. We are not limited by either time or space.

I believe in reading the Bible systematically and regularly. I find it far more meaningful to read an entire book, though not at one sitting, than to read individual texts. Having said that, I know that for the majority of us certain portions have become landmarks; we come back to them again and again. For example, when I think of prayer, I turn to the Gospels and those portions where we find Jesus at prayer. If, for the moment, the subject uppermost in my mind is healing, I turn to those places where Jesus and the disciples healed. I want, not only minute details, but to be captured by the spirit until as nearly as possible I am of the same mind.

I mark my Bible in various colors. I make marginal notes. I have even dated the time and place where I have read certain portions. When I return to them for quick glimpses, they are old friends on the trail of life.

But to read the Bible as one would study history or science is to miss out on something great and wonderful. Rather we read it to find a friend, one who will never let us down, who will walk with us through life and welcome us on that far shore in the light of a new day when we are assigned eternal roles. If we read it in that fashion, we will travel the trail to adventure across the centuries with a host of witnesses who have tested it thoroughly and found it dependable.

For the one just beginning to explore the life of the contemplative, I say, look to the psalms. Begin with what is probably the most familiar: "The Lord is my shepherd, I shall not want" (Ps. 23:1).

Now ask What is it I really want above all else? Remember, we shape our lives by the gods we choose.

Perhaps the greatest help in shaping our desires will be found in the psalms. The writers lived close to the powerful emotions of life—anger, desire, fear, failure, sin, repentance, suffering, happiness, uncertainty, death. For answers, they turned to God.

To make the study of the psalms easier, get a paperback edition that can be carried in a pocket, brief case, or purse. There will be many times along the way when one can refer to them. Read them thoughtfully with a marking pencil so that the ideas explored by the writer may become the basis for meditation and direction.

At the suggestion of Dr. Elton Trueblood, my wife, Rae, and I began reading the Bible in quite a different way.

We had always read a chapter at a time. Dr. Trueblood said if the New Testament were divided into eleven-verse segments the four Gospels and the Acts of the Apostles could be read in approximately one year. And so we began, using *Good News for Modern Man.* Chapters are sub-headed much like a newspaper; topics are printed in bold-face type. Usually we read only one topic each day, but if they were exceptionally short, we read a second. If there were questions, and often there were, we turned to a commentary. At times we compared the version we were reading with others. While we did not quibble over a word, it was surprising what a difference just changing a word or two could make.

Reading the Bible this way is like traveling on the Blue Ridge Parkway as it meanders mile-high, clinging to the backbone of the Blue Ridge Mountains. It is the scenic overviews every mile or so, rather than the forty-five miles per hour speed limit, that make it so relaxing. Each overlook is more thrilling than the last. One can spend hours up there in that rare and heady atmosphere drinking it all in; so it is with the Bible.

Along the way we encountered majestic thoughts and many old friends. Usually they hadn't changed. They were as we remembered them, but there were also some happy surprises, for suddenly we would meet a new acquaintance, one we were convinced we had never met before.

Because my work often took me far from home for several days at a time, we would plan ahead just what we would read each day we were apart. In that way we were together even though we were separated by as much as the width of a continent. Each day we dated and marked where that particular portion of Scripture was read.

Fortunately we were able to travel together a few times during those months. Now it is like a travelogue to look back and remember under what conditions a particular portion of Scripture was read—New Orleans; El Paso; Chicago; Minneapolis; Grand Island, Nebraska; Deadwood, South Dakota; Harbison, Delaware; Salem, Virginia; Miami; Sacramento. Some of them, according to marginal notations, we read in a hotel or motel, others in an airport. A few were read while we were driving along the highway.

And so we have wondered and wandered through the Bible, traveling slowly, taking many little by-paths to further explore an idea, yet all the while wondering at the great truths there for the taking. Each section of the Scriptures stimulates some special kind of interest just as does each section of the country, and we explored the Bible to the best of our ability, learning about its people, the culture, the geography, the triumphs and tragedies.

We looked carefully at the three basic thoughts of the Old Testament: God's promise to Abraham, God's covenant with the Hebrew nation, God's promise to David.

We thought long about those words, "In the beginning God . . ." They reminded us of the admonition in the psalms, "Unless the Lord builds the house, those who build it labor in vain" (Ps. 127:1). All things of lasting value begin with God.

We did not quarrel with science, nor did we argue about whether the universe was created in six twenty-four-hour days or six eons. For us it was enough that God had made it, and so we enjoyed and continue to enjoy its beauty, majesty, and wonder.

We did not find the variations in wording disturbing. Having been associated with newspaper and magazine writers for most of our lives, we realize that no two writers ever compose in the same fashion, and probably not for the same audience. We believe that biblical writers, whoever they were, were inspired by God, and so we accept the fact that "all scripture is inspired by God and profitable for teaching, for reproof, for correction, and for training in righteousness, that the man of God may be complete, equipped for every good work" (2 Tim. 3:16–17). If this is naïve, we plead guilty to being naïve. We find no quarrel with our liking for archaeology and geology; for us they go hand-in-hand with God's holy Word.

With that argument out of the way even before we began, we had the freedom to enjoy the Bible for what it is—God's message to man.

The travels of the Children of Israel in the wilderness are as packed with adventure as any story of early pioneers pushing westward with their covered wagons. The hardship, danger, doubt, courage, hope, birth, and death are all there. Sin is not glossed over. It is dark and ugly. The price it demands is high: "The wages of sin is death, but the free gift of God is eternal life in Christ Jesus our Lord" (Rom. 6:23).

The rise and fall of nations . . . again the implications are there. Unless a nation remains under God, freedom will have little value if it survives at all. Unless a people live in God, their living will have little security or permanence. But always there is hope: "If my people who are called by my name humble themselves, and pray and seek my face, and turn from their wicked ways, then I will hear from heaven, and will forgive their sin and heal their land" (2 Chron. 7:14).

We wondered about some pronouncements of the ancient prophets only to realize that history has fulfilled many of their predictions. Because of this we look forward expectantly to the eventual fulfillment of all God's promises.

The beauty, majesty, and human drama portrayed in the psalms, with their peaks and valleys of utter dejection and happy jubilation, are as true today as when they were first sung by the psalmist or penned on his parchment.

Recently I spent a happy afternoon with a couple in their eighties, Papa and Mama Mayes. They have spent their lives on a small Texas ranch. They know the discouragement of drought, the scourge of insects, the terror of wind and hail. They have seen depression and inflation. Children and grandchildren have been born, and some of them have gone off to war. But as they recounted these things, they held a Bible with well-marked pages.

Time after time I noticed the letters *T* and *P* before a verse. I questioned the meaning, and that wonderful lady replied, "Whenever we were facing a problem, we turned to one of God's promises and marked it with the letter *T*. That meant tried. We were standing firm on that promise. When it was fulfilled, the letter *P* was put there. That meant proven. Tried and proven."

For them, living consisted in making the words of Scripture their own by memorizing and repeating them with a deep and simple trust, knowing that the God they love is able.

Just as the long shadows of evening were lengthening around that ranch home when I drove away, so were the long shadows of life reaching around those wonderful folks, but the security and confidence they radiated were evidences of a home built with the help of the Lord and continued in his promise.

6. The End of the Rope

He said, "This is it. I'm at the end of my rope."

A dependable surgeon said, "When things go wrong, I wish people wouldn't get the idea that it is as final as a hole in the head."

Does some incident out of the past blight our today? Heartbreak, a moral misstep, a dream come to nought? Or is it dread of tomorrow?

Anxiety, fear, frustration, and sorrow are emotions common to all, and we must deal with them if life is to be experienced to the fullest. Financial disaster, the loss of a job, retirement, old age, a lump beneath the skin, failure in school, a bad marriage, a dead-end job, moving to a new location, loss of physical attractiveness, a loved one in peril

—any one of these can cloud the days and make the nights hideous. Anxieties can pop up at the most unexpected times and in the most unusual places, and they must be faced. But how?

Get quiet. Remember, emotion is not the real you. Emotion may scream that this is the end of everything, complete disaster, but the real you or me is that deep center where we experience union with God. He is there, still in control if we but let him take control. The visible world is sustained by the invisible. We move boldly from thoughts and feelings that are swamping us to Christ who is within us. We make an effort to release frustrations and look for ways to turn difficulties into steppingstones that will lead to victory.

A woman who suddenly lost her husband told how for a few hours she thought it was the end of everything. Their lives had been dependent on each other. Together they had planned so definitely for the future. Then she said she remembered the great promise: "Fear not, for I am with you, be not dismayed, for I am your God; I will strengthen you, I will help you, I will uphold you with my victorious right hand" (Isa. 41:10).

She said with that thought firmly fixed in her mind she determined not to make any big decisions for at least a year. She remained quietly in her home and in her church where she had friends. She made a careful inventory of her resources. She conferred with a friend she could trust. Eventually she sold her home, moved into an apartment, and found a job that soon became meaningful to her. At sixty she is making a new life for herself.

Fear paralyzes; quietness and a positive approach calm. Often in my moments of anxiety I turn to the story of Elisha's servant who awakened one morning and saw an enemy army and horses and chariots surrounding the city. In his fright he rushed to Elisha and asked, "What shall we do?" Elisha replied, "Don't be afraid for there are more with us than with them." Then Elisha prayed that his servant's eyes be opened. They were, and he saw the mountain was full of horses and chariots of fire to protect them (see 2 Kings 6:15–19).

With the mind stilled, begin with a prayer of affirmation: "I know you are a God of wisdom, love, peace, and power. Let this thing that is troubling me so greatly work out for the good of all concerned. If there are lessons to be learned, let me learn them. If there are mistakes to be forgiven and corrected, give me the strength and courage to take whatever measures should be taken and to trust you for the outcome."

Easier said than done! Yes, a loud yes from one who knows.

How do we release fears, anxieties, and frustrations which can have such an effect on our outer lives?

There, perhaps, is the clue—the outer life is not as important as the inner life, that calmness in the heart of a storm that refuses to be defeated. As long as we have the love and presence of God within, nothing can touch us too deeply to break our union with him. This thought we must keep uppermost: God is with me. His life fills me and strengthens me. His guiding presence is with me throughout the entire day and night. He never leaves; waking or sleeping, sick or well, we are surrounded and enfolded by the loving presence of God. It is easy to affirm this while sailing on smooth waters, but the great lesson we must learn is the practice of this awareness under any and all situations.

Sooner or later every person who would be freed from fears and anxieties must learn to stand alone with God. Seldom does this happen instantaneously. It takes time to cultivate an unwavering trust in God, but the time to begin is with the first anxious feeling. Do not delay. Affirm that

God is adequate for every situation. The more we practice this, the stronger our faith becomes. The more we affirm and the more we depend on God's promises, the sooner we find our faith in him unshakable, founded upon solid rock. We begin with him rather than fretting and fuming and wondering how to make things right. We turn from self and circumstances that would disturb and trust him completely. We claim the promise, "Thou dost keep him in perfect peace, whose mind is stayed on thee, because he trusts in thee" (Isa. 26:3).

We do not become frightened by lack of material things, the loss of work, or even the loss of a loved one. Not only is God able to provide everything we need in abundance, but he has given us a spiritual strength that is even stronger than physical strength. We build upon the best we have within us (the presence of God) and use it to find a new world of accomplishment with peace and love. Consequently, if there is some positive action we are to take, we will be enabled to do so with calm assurance.

After turning to him, we need to ascertain to the best of our ability whether the threat to our security and peace of mind is real or only a mere possibility, a figment of imagination. We often borrow troubles by letting our imagination run rampant.

If you are a perpetual worrier, begin by making a list of all the things that nag at you, keep you awake, spoil your pleasure, and erode your quiet times. I would venture to say that fully one-half of them are worries that never happen. More than 25 percent will concern past events about which you can do nothing. Such a list kept honestly for the period of a year will reveal that less than 10 percent were real enough to worry about.

But suppose it isn't imagination. Financial disaster is certain, the loss of a job is sure, retirement is imminent. This is the time to take stock of ourself and our resources, limited though they be, and ask, What more than anything would I like to do? This may be the golden opportunity to live some dreams.

A woman in her midsixties, her family grown, her husband retired, found she was losing her zest for parties and teas. Nor were there extra funds for travel or other expensive hobbies. Having always cherished a secret ambition to be a nurse, she became a volunteer in a large hospital and found complete fulfillment.

A seeming disaster may be the golden opportunity to live some dreams. With nothing to lose and everything to gain, perhaps this is the time to launch out, to make an adventure of living, to say with Robert Browning:

> Grow old along with me!
> The best is yet to be,
> The last of life, for which the first was made:
> Our times are in his hand
> Who saith, "A whole I planned,
> Youth shows but half; trust God: see all nor be afraid!"
> From *Rabbi Ben Ezra*

Before we move however, we make sure it is the type of undertaking on which we can ask God's blessing.

If there is a malignancy or other serious condition, have we obtained the best medical advice available? Medical science is making some great breakthroughs. In the words of the surgeon, "It may not be as final as a hole in the head." No matter how desperate the situation, with God nothing is impossible. Never think of any condition as beyond God's help. Instead, turn to him and sincerely ask for healing, in faith believing that he is able, that he made every cell of our body and knows our needs. Then with every confidence turn back to life, resolving to make every day count and trusting him for the outcome.

Whenever disaster looms, it is well to read Exodus 14. Disaster was hard on the heels of the Children of Israel when Moses said to them, "Fear not, stand firm, and see the salvation of the Lord" (Exod. 14:13). This is the time to stand still both physically and mentally, to stop the uncontrolled, racing thoughts, to settle down inwardly, to turn away from self-pity, and to recall that the presence of God is with you, working diligently for your good. Say again and again, "He is able," and believe it with every fiber of your body.

I believe in prayer for healing just as I believe in medical doctors and hospitals. They go hand-in-hand. Our family has been blessed for more than twenty years with a wonderful, skillful surgeon, Dr. Edmund Benz. He has seen us through long periods of severe illness, but great as is his skill, we appreciate even more his Christian compassion and understanding. Yet a doctor can do only so much. To assure victory, he needs the cooperation, determination, and faith of the patient, not only in medicine, but in the Great Physician.

There is a simple prayer for healing anyone can say: "Cleanse me and use me as you will." I can pray that with confidence. It is a full-grown petition that definitely commits one to be used of God; yet it in no sense implies making a deal. It implies that we believe there is a purpose for us and that we are willing to fulfill that purpose.

Too many of our prayers are little more than wishful mumbling. We expect nothing and we receive nothing. To receive, we must come to God in perfect confidence; yet if we are in any way at fault or if there are changes necessary, it is up to us to assume that responsibility. Sickness is often like sin; we enjoy it too much to give it up. Therefore, while we may pray, we have no intention of doing our part.

The scriptures tell us of thirty-three miracles performed by our Lord. Of that number, twenty-four had to do with healing. Time after time, Jesus talked of two things—forgiveness and action. Your sins are forgiven . . . take up your bed . . . go wash . . . go show yourself. Forgiveness, cleansing, and freeing, by whatever name, are ways of asking to be relieved of something. It may be a condition brought about as a result of our own actions or thinking. It may be something over which we have no control. Whatever it is, we are asking to be relieved of the suffering or the illness that is troubling us, not just for our own sake, but that we may truly be useful in God's kingdom.

Never should this or any prayer be uttered lightly, but it can be prayed as often as we think of it, perhaps the more often the better, for it reminds us of God's presence and of our dependence upon him.

Jan van Ruysbroeck, the fourteenth-century Flemish mystic, wrote: "The first and highest unity of man is in God; for all creatures depend upon this unity for their being, their life, and their preservation; and if they be separated in this wise from God, they fall into the nothingness and become naught. This unity is in us essentially, by nature, whether we be good or evil. And without our own working it makes us neither holy nor blessed. This unity we possess within us and yet above us, as the ground and the preserver of our being and of our life."

The ultimate hope for all of us, regardless of age, is moving from life to Life. While the outer person may fade, the inner—the divine presence—is endless life. Jesus said, "Let not your hearts be troubled; believe in God, believe also in me. In my Father's house are many rooms; if it were not so, would I have told you that I go to prepare a place for you?" (John 14:1-2).

Victor Hugo wrote: "The tomb is not a blind alley; it

is a thoroughfare. It closes upon the twilight, but it opens upon the dawn."

We all know that we must eventually die; still few of us accept it eagerly when the time comes. There is still an unknown, and we are prone to cling to the known as long as possible, and why not? If we are needed, if there is love to be shared, we want to fulfill our responsibility as well and able persons.

Perhaps one of life's most traumatic moments is reserved for the one who hears the physician say, "Six months to a year . . . eighteen months at the most . . ." Suffering, depression, and anxiety can be constant companions for one who has received such a sentence.

A banker friend was sharing an experience he had working with a man who had been told he had not more than three months to live.

I exclaimed, "How terrible."

The banker said, "Not really. It is terrible when a person is wiped out suddenly without time to make preparation. This man has opportunity to put his house in order in every respect and prepare his loved ones. His task is to make every day count. If he does that, trusting God all the way . . ." He smiled. "I hope I have that much warning."

Even in the direst circumstances all things are possible with the one who first put the breath of life into our being.

Fortunately, not all anxieties are of this magnitude. Perhaps it is failure in school. You are not the first. But why? Can the blame be pinpointed? Can something be done about it? Perhaps not right now, but in the future? Many a person has failed once, even twice, then found himself or herself and come back stronger than ever.

Determination and courage are tremendous attributes to cultivate when facing adversity, and these smouldering embers can be fanned into open flame with expectancy. If we only believe, great things can happen! We live in the age of miracles. Why not expect one?

Moving to a new location can be very upsetting; yet one-fourth of the population will move this year, and not all will move to the most desirable location. However, there is no place, no matter how drab, that does not have some attractiveness. Discover what it is, small though it be, and capitalize on it. It may be that God is opening an entirely new life in a new place with new friends and new opportunities. Change is a part of life. It is living and growing.

Loss of physical attractiveness! None of us wants that, but sooner or later it comes to most. Nevertheless, sometimes the person who is most unattractive at first glance has a warmth of personality that can become sheer magnetism. Think of some great men and women of history who were physically unattractive but went on to places of prominence and achievement. However, it may be that only the loss of a few pounds, a change of diet, some corrective exercises, or a little more attention to grooming is all that is necessary. Whatever it is, if we let God's presence truly radiate from us with warmth and love, there will be a charm that captivates.

With courage and determination even the greatest handicaps have been overcome. Before he was thirty years old, Beethoven was losing his hearing; yet he went on to give the world some of its greatest symphonies. In the darkness of his blindness John Milton wrote *Paradise Lost*. John Bunyan wrote *Pilgrim's Progress* in the starkness of a prison cell. In a similar situation the Apostle Paul wrote his great letters which now are a portion of the New Testament.

Remembering that our body is the temple of the living God should be enough incentive to send us on the trip of trips. Rather than concentrating on our bodies alone, we concentrate on God and glorify him with our bodies. Consequently we will not abuse them. We will treat them as truly wonderful gifts from him, knowing if we trust him he will supply all our needs.

What about a bad marriage? As always, twenty-twenty hindsight is easier than twenty-twenty foresight. Persons entering any partnership agreement should carefully consider God's guidelines: "Unless the Lord builds the house, those who build it labor in vain" (Ps. 127:1).

Still these warnings have been ignored. The mistake has been made. The little foxes are really nibbling—pettiness, argument, long silences, mistrust. If the house has not completely collapsed, perhaps a good repair job can save it. After a divorce many admit they could have made a go of it with a little more effort on the part of one or both, but often one has to initiate the repairs and even carry the burden.

Too often we feel it is our life, the problem is of our own making; therefore, we must work it out by ourself. Such an attitude is a grave fallacy. This may be the time for humble confession: "Lord, I made this mistake. I have no one to blame. I do not know what is right at this point, but I leave the direction and outcome entirely to you. To the best of my ability I will follow your leading."

It is often liberating to let someone else carry the burden. Many times the thing that stands between us and our good is our inability to trust the problem to one who is able. Without realizing it, we could be actually afraid to let go and trust God for the decision.

If, however, the marriage has crashed, everything possible has been done to save it and it still has failed, perhaps this is the beginning. The end of human effort is where God sometimes begins. When the human steps aside, admits total defeat, God, the omnipotent, the unbeatable, is still right on the job.

No matter how dark the night or how great the failure, the presence of God will give us courage to begin again.

Dreams may have come to nought, but all is not lost. We can go forward into newness of life, move out of the deep shadows into the sunlight of his love, and find fulfillment.

Anxiety is not always for self; often it is for a loved one. We are troubled, trying desperately to come up with a solution, and up to the moment have failed, perhaps have been rejected by the one we so want to help. We feel a tremendous sense of responsibility. We continue to argue, "There must be something I can do," when in reality there is only one thing we can do—release the person and the situation to God.

This is the time to hold fast to our faith in the power of God, repeating over and over, "He is able. He is able."

Just as we pray from the depths of our soul for self, so we pray for another. "Lord, you know I trust myself to you, and so I trust this loved one to your care. I know you are strong and I am weak, that you are able where I am unable. I know you have the solution if I will but step aside and let you have your way. I am thankful I can turn this over to you. I am giving all my anxieties to you, for I know you do care. Now let us both experience the promise of the Master when he said, 'Peace I leave with you; my peace I give to you; not as the world gives do I give to you. Let not your hearts be troubled, neither let them be afraid' (John 14:27)."

This is a good time to picture the quiet pool at the foot of the rapids. How wonderful it is to rest in still waters and thank God for the quietness that comes in trust and obedience.

While resting in this calm, ask an important question, Am I just borrowing trouble? Does this concern belong to today, or is it something that may or may not happen in the future? This does not mean we should not plan for the future and make necessary provision for it physically, financially, and psychologically. But we should not worry about it.

Jesus said, "Do not be anxious about tomorrow, for tomorrow will be anxious for itself. Let the day's own trouble be sufficient for the day" (Matt. 6:34).

Perhaps more than anything this great teaching of Jesus is saying that we have a source of inner strength from God that can see us through present difficult times, but not to worry about the future, that when the time comes he will supply the needed strength.

In his great prayer the Master said, "Give us this day our daily bread" (Matt. 6:11). Never once did he tell us to pray for tomorrow's needs.

As we think of these promises and stand firm with them, we should remember that our Lord does not say he will deliver us from effort, uncertainty, the strain of our jobs, or family and individual problems. He does promise a source of strength to help our human capabilities meet life head-on and victoriously regardless of what it may throw at us.

God has given us the power to become whatever we should become. If we wish to be joyous, creative, serving persons, facing daily problems with confidence, we release self to him and say, "Lord, while these circumstances seem beyond my control, with your help I shall overcome if you will show me what to do." Then we listen to the still, small voice within.

Prayer is not an escape hatch. It is our responsibility to become all that God has planned for us; so with confidence we picture a radiant, successful, trusting person, and with every thought and action we move in that direction.

At the end of the rope—tie a knot in it and hang on, but not alone. The great promise of our Lord is "I am with you always, to the close of the age" (Matt. 28:20).

7. A Welcome Companion

A tremendous thought releases us from all fear, anxiety, want, and loneliness and knows only peace, security, and prosperity—"In him we live and move and have our being" (Acts 17:28). In whom? Why in the creator of the universe, the one who flung the stars in place. We are in him, and he is in us.

How do we recognize this oneness? By getting quiet and accepting it, then living it with every thought, word, and deed, not by ourselves, but by letting him live in us, through us, and with us. Union is achieved when effort stops and faith takes its place. It is not something we experience just in high moments of resolve or at a spiritual retreat but all the time, even in the humdrum, only there is no humdrum. There is born a life so full, so creative, that even though we are sitting still there is still constant achievement.

Two accounts in the Bible are a never-ending source of delight and inspiration for me. One is the visit of Jesus to the home of Mary and Martha (see Luke 10:38–42). The other is his walk with the two men on the road to Emmaus and his visit in their home (Luke 24:13–30).

In both instances Jesus was real to those folks. He listened to them, talked with them, and shared with them. He was a welcome companion, mingling with them. Upon occasion, I like to picture him sitting across the room from me or walking with me. There are times when we talk, but more often we are like two long-time friends sitting by a campfire at night. The silence of the wilderness is all around us, and we too are silent, thinking long thoughts as people do in such surroundings.

I do not know what Jesus looked like. I can imagine, and that is all; still it helps to visualize a presence, one who understands. Without words, our thoughts intermingle, and he influences me. To be constantly aware of his presence makes one unafraid of the world.

There is not a flower that blossoms, not a seed that becomes a plant, not a bird that sings, not a sunset or a sunrise flaming across the sky that does not proclaim his presence. By the very acts of nature, by the love I receive and give, I am assured that he is always near whether during the rush hours of life or in the quiet of the home when I listen to a great oratorio. Even though I travel to strange places, fly in airplanes, or go down in submarines, he is there.

Paul, writing to his friends at Corinth, said, "Do you not realize that Jesus Christ is in you?" (2 Cor. 13:5).

Our Lord makes himself known in many ways; yet because of our preconceived ideas about him, where he is and how he acts, we do not find him. Often we are looking

73

off in the distance to some future event and fail to see him in everyday experiences. It is when we are open and receptive that he makes his presence known, even in the most unexpected places and times.

It is we who limit God. Almost from babyhood we have been drawing up our own set of specifications for him, thereby shutting out the wonders that could be ours.

If only we could realize that we do not have to accomplish great things or be something we are not to have a place in his love. All we have to do is be ourselves where we are and listen. Regardless of our station in life, we have the ability to grow in a vital and wonderful way because the spirit of God is within us.

Our Lord said, "The kingdom of God is within you" (Luke 17:21 KJV). His kingdom is joy, peace, and security in the Holy Spirit, but to have this sense of his presence we must prepare a place and keep it worthy of him. For that he gave direction when he said, "If a man loves me, he will keep my word, and my Father will love him, and we will come to him and make our home with him" (John 14:23).

This is the best news we can have; we are not alone, not hunting an elusive spirit. He is with us and wants to be recognized even more than we may want to recognize him. He has a divine plan for every life based on the divine order of the universe. The plan he has for us will not harm another, will in no way move another from his or her rightful place, but it will blend us in harmony and purpose if we let it. His plan has been thought out well in advance. His spirit is in us to administer that plan, but he must have our willingness. When he has that, he will supply all the power in the universe.

We are never closer to God or more involved with life than when we let him have his way with us, love us, serve us, direct us, and work through us.

"And if you obey the voice of the Lord your God, being

careful to do all his commandments which I command you this day, the Lord your God will set you high above all nations of the earth. And all these blessings shall come upon you and overtake you, if you obey the voice of the Lord your God" (Deut. 28:1–2).

This I believe was the secret of the master teacher. He completely fulfilled those requirements. He supplied the willingness; God supplied the power. This was the secret he attempted to pass on to his followers and is still trying to pass on to you and me today. God himself will work at the very heart of our lives, taking increasing control as we become more and more willing to let him. When we cease trying to make self the supreme architect and let God do the planning, life assumes the right direction and purpose.

But we cry out, "I want to be free. I want to be liberated. I want to make my own choices."

True, choice is freedom. If we were not free to choose, we would in no wise be free. But here we have choice— self or God. We find perfect freedom when we choose God—freedom from fear, want, and loneliness. We lose it when we choose self and the bondage it brings. Christian freedom means trusting God rather than trusting self or the world. It is security rather than futility. Here we would remember the two builders. One built his house on sand, and when the storm came, it collapsed. The other built his house upon rock, and it withstood the torrents (see Luke 6:46–49). Never think the Sermon on the Mount or the other teachings of Jesus are mere idealistic philosophies; they are a true analysis of correct decisions.

Scarcely a day goes by that we are not faced with a new task, a new challenge, or a new opportunity. Sometimes it may seem beyond our capabilities, but when we let God take over and furnish the strength and direction while we supply the trust and willingness, great things are accomplished, and obstacles become opportunities. The indwell-

1ng of his spirit gives us courage and confidence. It lifts us to higher levels of living and attainment, and we become living witnesses for him.

No matter how busy we are, how pressed for time, a moment spent in thinking about our oneness with a loving, sharing God erases the little worries and doubts that threaten to take over. Within us the unlimited power of God is there to support us just as any loving father will support a child. We have the opportunity to be all that we are intended to be. If God is in us, he does not come and go. He is with us constantly in sickness and in health, in sorrow and in joy. Through our union with him we are filled with courage and enthusiasm that supplies rather than saps energy as do fears and loneliness. Our thoughts focus on his order, not on the disorder of the world. Our oneness with him renews and strengthens.

When we claim his presence, we are asserting our faith. We are testifying that we know he cares enough about us to be with us. Any obstacle in our life, any discouragement, should be a reminder that we need to walk more closely with him. The more we depend on him, the more we find him.

Through an awareness of his presence within, his companionship, we are able to meet any situation with confidence and peace we find in no other way. This behooves us to establish mental habits of turning to God even when demands are greatest. Perhaps the big difference in the saints and in us is that they are careful to remind themselves that God is with them, and they are constantly responsive to his voice.

How great it is to awaken to a new day and affirm, "God, you watched over me while I slept. I know you will be with me throughout the busy day."

Along the way will come doubts, fears, temptations. This is the time to pray, "Almighty God, unto whom all hearts are open, all desires known, and from whom no secrets are hid; Cleanse the thoughts of our hearts by the inspiration of thy Holy Spirit, that we may perfectly love thee, and worthily magnify thy holy Name; through Christ our Lord" (from the *Book of Common Prayer*).

The voice assures us that what others can do we too can do. The disciples were ordinary men, but they met an extraordinary person, Jesus Christ. Their weakness was turned into strength; their doubts, into confidence; their fear, into courage; their life, into a light that has shown across the centuries. With these thoughts uppermost, we resolve to do four things:

1. To let God have total authority for the direction of our life. The Apostle Paul wrote to his friends at Rome, "If the Spirit of him who raised Jesus from the dead dwells in you, he who raised Christ Jesus from the dead will give life to your mortal bodies also through his Spirit which dwells in you" (Rom. 8:11).

As we think of these words, we would close our inner being to both outer and inner distractions, either of which would call us away from him and back to ourselves. This is the time to lose sight of all side issues and lesser things and remember one thing—the presence of God. What I am suggesting is the secret practice of turning inward to the presence so there is constant realization and communication even though we are busy in the world of daily affairs. Even at mealtime, in the busiest of places with clamor and noise all about, we can lift our hearts up to him, and this slightest remembrance will bring him even closer.

2. To endeavor at all times to practice the simple courtesy of Christ in contacts with all others. Never did Christ hold another up to ridicule or scorn. Never did he belittle

a person. Always he held out a helping, healing, forgiving hand. Never did he look upon himself as either holier or better because of his uniqueness; instead he took the basin and towel and assumed the lowliest position. If we would bring our lives into conformity with his, we would behave under all circumstances as he did. He had no other desire than to do his Father's will.

3. To become a channel through which the love of God can flow into the lives of others. The follower of the master teacher allows his or her being to be filled with the very spirit of God—his love, concern, and wisdom—and then let that spirit flow into the lives of others, bettering them because of the contact.

By our example we would call others to be still and listen, to realize God's love is for all. Our task is to encourage others to stop their incessant running around in a wild search for something and to open the door to the one who would come into their lives and dwell with them. Too many well-intentioned people are so busy with their efforts to do and to achieve that they fail to hear God asking what he might do for them. The great theme of Christianity is not that we have loved God but that God first loved us.

4. Then expect it to happen. Faith is the way in which we advance on our journey toward union with God. "Call to me and I will answer you, and will tell you great and hidden things which you have not known" (Jer. 33:3).

This holy presence is mysterious and inexplainable. It cannot be accurately described; yet it is there for one who would listen and obey. In this center we are Christ's and he is ours, and because he is God's, we too are God's. This indwelling of the Holy Spirit is not reserved for a select few; it is for all who would seriously turn their lives over to him without reservation until the inner life becomes a holy sanctuary of trust and praise where our minds are kept in perpetual recognition of him. As such an experience becomes ours, we can say with the prophet, "In returning and rest you shall be saved; in quietness and in trust shall be your strength" (Isa. 30:15).

To lead a life of high adventure, try God.

8. Knapsacks

Knapsacks of every color and description have become very popular. They appear on city streets, on the college campus, and in the office as well as in the wilderness. Actually we are all knapsack carriers. Going through life we add to them bit by bit, seldom discarding but tucking in an item here, another there, until we stagger beneath the burden, reluctant to discard anything.

A magazine cartoon showed a woman standing in the middle of her crowded attic. Her comment, "I'm glad I can't take it with me. It's the only way I'll ever get rid of all this."

Some years ago, with several others, I was at the jump-off for an extended canoe trek into the Canadian wilderness.

Our guide said, "I want you to take all your belongings, spread them out on the floor, then divide them into three piles. Put those things you consider an absolute necessity in one pile, those you would like to have in a second, and those you can leave behind in a third. Remember, there will be some long portages where an ounce will feel like a pound and a pound becomes a ton."

We began to sort while the guide sat quietly off to one side of the room. When we had finished he came over and surveyed the various piles, not those we were going to leave behind, or the things we would like to have; his attention was centered on the pile we felt to be an absolute necessity.

From mine he discarded an extra shirt, a pair of pants, a pair of shoes.

"But the ones I am wearing will get wet, perhaps torn," I protested.

"They'll dry," he said. "If something rips, we've got a needle and thread."

For a long time now I have watched people come into bus depots and airports, some of them burdened with baggage, while others, the experienced, are so casual, so unencumbered. Recently a well-known columnist wrote she could go to Europe with a change of undies and a toothbrush.

Perhaps if there is any one motto we should keep uppermost in our minds it would be simplify, simplify, simplify.

A successful businessman gives this advice: Before purchasing anything ask, Do I really need it, or do I just want it? Then wait three days before making the final decision.

One can play an interesting little game by walking through the home and deciding how many things would be replaced if what we have were lost or destroyed. Knicknacks, gadgets, appliances, books, ornaments, and clothes are nice, but do we really need them? Or did we acquire them on the spur of the moment?

On one occasion I was entertained in two homes on successive evenings. In the first, the table was laden with beautiful dishes, glassware, and silver. There were too many kinds of food to count. Throughout the meal the hostess kept jumping up and rushing to the kitchen to get something more. Her big desire was to see that her guest had enough and to spare. As food was passed and repassed, there was little time for conversation, and what there was was interrupted and dull. Not until the meal was finished did the hostess remember we had not said grace.

The next evening was quite different. The home was the kind where one felt a simple peace. The manners of the host and hostess were impeccable; their voices, low and agreeable. There were a minimum of dishes; the food was plain but delicious. Not once did the hostess leave the dining room. There was plenty of time for grace. The conversation was built around great ideas and continued well into the evening. It was a time memorable both for its simplicity and true enjoyment.

Now this does not apply to material possessions only. There is the matter of one's schedule—committee meetings, planning sessions, unnecessary running to and fro, the search for pleasure, for excitement.

Recently I heard a young pastor on the short side of thirty preach a sermon that made a lasting impression: "If This Were My Year." He told that early in the week he had been out in the church cemetery. There he had looked at the grave markers with their dates and had asked himself, "If this were my year, what changes would I make, what things would become unnecessary, and what would assume places of paramount importance?" And then he told of spending another day in a meeting. He said, "If I knew this were my year, I would not waste time in all the meetings that jam my schedule, rob my family and my parishioners of my time, take me away from my study, and cause me to neglect those moments I need with my Lord." He concluded by saying, "I am going to rearrange my schedule. There are many things that can and will be eliminated, but there will also be those, the better, which are added."

I recalled John Woolman had said something about meetings in his journal. That night I checked it. In 1758 the good Quaker wrote: "I had occasion to consider that it is a weighty thing to speak much in large meetings for business, except our minds are rightly prepared and we clearly understand the case we speak to, instead of forwarding, we hinder business and make more labor for those on whom the burden of work is laid. If selfish views or a partial spirit have any room in our minds, we are unfit for the Lord's work; if we have a clear prospect of the business and proper weight on our minds to speak, we should avoid useless apologies and repetitions."

A professional man says at the beginning of the year he marks his date book with birthdays, anniversaries, and holidays that rightfully belong to his family. If he is asked to make other appointments for those times, he replies that he is already scheduled and makes no further explanation. Likewise, each day he sets aside time for his wife and children and a time for devotion and meditation.

Material wants and time schedules undoubtedly both need overhauling, but perhaps there is even a greater stumbling block—our attitudes.

A man in a large organization is forever saying, "Now I expect they are going to be unhappy about this, and when they come up with their objections, I am going to be ready for them." Then he spends hours planning what he will say and do if the issue is ever raised. Fortunately, the majority of them never are, but since he is always looking ahead, he never has time to be at rest or to be creative. His mind is in a constant strategy meeting, preparing for battles, most of which will never be fought.

A professional woman has kept an extensive diary for years. In it she has recorded few happy experiences. Mostly she has recorded conversations and events, especially if she feels an unfairness or a slight has been directed toward her. Her explanation is that she is going to be ready if the time ever comes . . .

Some persons are supersensitive. They almost seem to look for slights. They blow the least little thing out of proportion. However, the person who has made this a lifetime habit can change with a bit of effort.

Irritation, resentment, and hurt feelings can be tuned out by substituting thoughts of peace and good will. These emotions are not the real person, the Christ within; rather they come and go like electric current in transmission lines. Electricity is wonderful, but it can be destructive unless controlled. So it is with our emotions.

A neighbor, who often stops in for a cup of coffee and to exchange a book and some good conversation, has been telling of a new discovery, the result of something he read. He says there was a time when his mind was filled with disturbing thoughts and his nights were often sleepless. Now he begins to prepare for bed by programming his mind with thoughts of all the wonderful things he expects to accomplish the next day and the resultant good which may take place. He thinks new ideas. He remembers that Christ is renewing him body and soul, that he has plans for him. He says since doing that he is usually wide awake before the alarm sounds, anxious to be up and about, his mind filled with happy, creative thoughts. And he adds, a great day is the result. Possibilities he might never have recognized are just waiting to be seized.

Whether we realize it or not, the majority of us must deal with two conflicting elements in our lives if we are to realize our true potential—the plus factor and the minus factor, positive and negative.

Paul wrote to his young friend Timothy: "For God did not give us a spirit of timidity—of cowardice, of craven and cringing and fawning fear—but [He has given us a spirit] of power and of love and of calm *and* well-balanced mind *and* discipline *and* self-control" (2 Tim. 1:7, Amplified).

In a real way Paul was saying, realize your plus factor. Start now. Don't be afraid. Reach out for accomplishment, health, and a life of service and opportunity. If you are governed by fears and a sense of failure, that is exactly what life will deal to you—rejection and disappointment. If you center your attention on the true gift God has given you—power and calm courage—you may reach out and claim the good that is already yours. If you have ability and talent, use it with vigor so that both others and you may profit by it. Always keep this plus factor uppermost in your mind. Launch out and do whatever God has given you to do. If you have never quite made it before, forget it. Perhaps you were concentrating too much on the minus factor. Remember, it is your plus factor that God wants you to use. If this factor controls you, you are on the way.

In our moments of quietness it may be well to take inventory. Are our lives burdened with the minus factor—failure, bitterness, worry, possible retaliation and revenge—or are they filled with the plus factor—happy expectancy, courage, accomplishment? Perhaps we all need to decide what we will carry in our knapsacks.

A knapsack filled with love, trust, faith, hope, the memory of warm friendships, good books, glorious sunsets, great hymns of faith, the smile of little children, and the simple trust of a faithful pet is never a burden even on the most difficult portages. Rather these contents tend to smooth the path and make us welcome companions, not only for others, but for ourselves, and they send us on to true accomplishment.

9. Riptides

As we delve deeper into quietness, riptides may threaten to pull us under, for the novelty wears off. At first it is fairly smooth going, but after a few attempts with little progress, there come times of doubt, discouragement, and guilt, especially if we pray, "Search me, O God, and know my heart! Try me and know my thoughts! And see if there be any wicked way in me, and lead me in the way everlasting!" (Ps. 139:23–24). This is when disturbing thoughts take over if given the opportunity. In effect, we have asked God to hold up a mirror so that we may see ourselves as he sees us, not only with all our imperfections, but with our greater possibilities if we are willing to undergo the rigors of self-discipline.

Every rational person basically knows the difference between right and wrong in terms of the larger issues such as stealing, killing, and wanton destruction. But in the past we have shrugged off comparatively minor offenses, rationalizing that everyone lives with them.

For each person the list will be different; yet there is no avoiding these disturbing forces until they are removed if one is to experience union with God. A person makes room for God only by wiping away all smudges and smears and uniting his or her will with the perfect will of God. Unwelcome thoughts are present and continue to disturb and pull until the condition is corrected by confession, change, and, often, restitution. Jesus said, "So if you are offering your gift at the altar, and there remember that your brother has something against you, leave your gift there before the altar and go; first be reconciled to your brother, and then come and offer your gift" (Matt. 5:23–24). To put it bluntly, there can be no peace until forgiveness and reconciliation are complete.

Perhaps the forces which most frequently run counter to our longing for peace and oneness with God are pride, haughtiness, self-righteousness, anger, resentment, fear, worry, inferiority, busyness, and idols. These forces deny God's love and prohibit our full acceptance of it. Time after time as we seek union with him, we feel them tugging at us, disturbing us, and blocking our oneness because oneness depends on openness and harmony with his purpose. Any of these attitudes brings a jarring discord to his way of life. To be out of harmony with God is to be out of harmony with others and with self.

Not only does lack of harmony rob us of complete union with God, but like an infected sore, it eats away at us, festers, and torments. It feeds poison into our system and robs us of a happy, effective approach to life and hours of needed sleep. It hampers digestion and limits creativeness. Perhaps no one will ever know how much sickness, loss of friends, lack of advancement, break-up of families, and finally complete self-destruction have been caused by harboring one or more of these attitudes. We may try to smother, forget, and rationalize them, but all these approaches are doomed to fail. These attitudes demand radical surgery that begins with confession to God and a plea for forgiveness; yet often when we sin, we try to hide. We try to escape from the one to whom we should turn just as we would turn to a dependable physician in time of critical illness.

To break out of the prison of habit and desire that has captured us is never easy, but to hold fast to the wrong is to suffer the torture and affliction of one held captive by a ruthless enemy. Life, as God would have us live it, is meant to be redemptive, creative, and joyful; the goal is not the prison of sin or the grave of defeat. With his help we can reshape life in accordance with his purpose and come out of a bad experience a stronger, better person.

This calls for discipline on our part, a new life-style to proclaim that we are his followers. Life is more than mere words. Life is living, not with wild abandon, but with disciplined purpose and direction.

To be tempted is one thing; to yield is another. Temptation comes at our most vulnerable point. In competition an opposing athlete, a debater, or an attorney always looks for his or her opponent's weakest point and launches the heaviest assault in that direction. So it is with temptation. Many times temptation catches us by surprise. It probes, nags, and torments; it becomes attractive, alluring. It says, "Just once. Others are doing it. Look at the fun." Above all, it is subtle.

In our quiet time we not only confess our wrongdoings, but we talk over our temptations with one who understands. True prayer, especially prayer for forgiveness and help, is secret correspondence with God. We can become completely open, not glossing over the most minute detail, telling him everything and seeking a way out. For that we must rely on the still, small voice within, for few of us are fortunate enough to have a prophet as did King David when Nathan went to him after he had been with Bathsheba and confronted him with the enormity of his sin (see 2 Sam. 12:1–23).

After that confrontation, heart-broken David prayed, "Have mercy on me, O God, according to thy steadfast love; according to thy abundant mercy blot out my transgressions. Wash me thoroughly from my iniquity, and cleanse me from my sin! For I know my transgressions, and my sin is ever before me. Against thee, thee only, have I sinned, and done that which is evil in thy sight" (Ps. 51:1–4).

Because all sin is first against God, then against another or self, we turn first to him for forgiveness. We ask him to cleanse the thoughts of our minds by the inspiration of his Holy Spirit; having done that, we begin to make restitution if it's necessary and at all possible.

Often to go to another, admit our wrong, and ask forgiveness is even harder than admitting it to God. It is a blow to our pride. It humbles us, and often we try to avoid such a confrontation, but there is no other way. The sooner done, the sooner the disturbance is removed.

Most of us would agree with the spiritual, "Lord, I Want to Be a Christian in My Heart"; yet we hesitate to take the step, thinking if we wait long enough the problem will disappear. So we put off this step and the thought of really changing our ways. Frankly, we may be getting a certain enjoyment out of our sins even though they disturb us at times. Often, we do not change until the disturbance becomes too great for us to handle. Because only God and we know our inner thoughts, we need to look inward, honestly put our thinking in perspective, and ask, Do I truly want forgiveness enough to change?

Perhaps we first need to consider some changes we

would have to make. If we admire a person who speaks plainly, then we must admire Jesus, for he was speaking plainly and directly when he said, "No one can serve two masters; for either he will hate the one and love the other, or he will be devoted to one and despise the other. You cannot serve God and mammon" (Matt. 6:24).

Jesus knew well that any sin pulls us away from God; it exerts a force that reaches into the heart of our being. It is like a sickness that is deep in the marrow of one's bones, hurting, destroying. It means estrangement from God, from others, and from self until it is corrected. As long as we let it, sin will be our master and our god even though it be a hated ruler.

Seldom does any one sin stand alone. Almost always others are involved. To practice any of them brings guilt feelings, and guilt can devastate our spirit of quietness. Usually the fear of being found out leads to untruthfulness and hypocrisy, a need to cover our tracks.

Selfishness and envy are generally associated with idols. We want something so much it assumes unnatural proportions and thus becomes an idol. We may be willing to pay any price for prestige, money, advancement, friends, or acceptance, and that price may be the loss of self-respect which leads to a feeling of inferiority.

With all these there is also worry, a termite that eats away day and night without ceasing until our destruction is complete. In our agony we cry out as did the writer of Lamentations, "My soul is bereft of peace, I have forgotten what happiness is" (Lam. 3:17).

As we struggle—and have no doubt about it, there usually is struggle—we need to ask as did Joseph when tempted by Potiphar's wife, "How then can I do this great wickedness, and sin against God?" (Gen. 39:9).

As we ask this question, it suddenly becomes more than just our problem alone.

It is also God's problem, and so we turn to him for the

necessary strength and courage to correct the wrong. We do not have to do it alone; in fact, we probably cannot do it without God's help. Our problems are not unique, and we are not the first to be so burdened. God is neither stampeded nor baffled by our frantic efforts. What we need most is to remember that our strength lies in quietness and confidence, not in frantic action. Our approach is to trust him. Job could say, "Though he slay me, yet will I trust in him" (Job 13:15, KJV).

One may say, "But if I confess, think of the consequences for myself, my family, my friends." There are times when confession need be made only to God and then forgotten, but if open confession is required, it may mean a period of suffering. Surgery is often a time of suffering, but God is the great physician.

As we ask forgiveness and courage, we remember that when we call upon God he is ready to forgive and stand by. This readiness overflows from his heart into ours and in the end makes us want to be forgiven as much as God wants to forgive. The question, however, is not one of getting God's forgiveness; the problem is our acceptance of it and the conditions it may impose upon us.

How do we understand and accept God's pardon? Do we completely accept it or do we continue to burden ourselves with needless guilt by remembering our transgressions, debating if they have truly been forgiven. Three times in Scripture our Lord's promise is stated almost in the same way: "I will forgive their iniquity, and I will remember their sins no more" (see Jer. 31:34, Heb. 8:12, Heb. 10:17). If this is his promise, can we do less than forget?

If we take this promise at face value, there is no longer a place for fear or guilt.

If an honest change has been made, there can no longer be doubt in the mind of one who has completely confessed and resolved to do nothing that cannot be done openly in the sight of God. However, the world may not be as ready to forgive as is God. There may be a penalty to pay, but as we reach up to him, he reaches down to us. When one is ready to trust and obey him, a little effort goes a long way. An inmate serving a long sentence for murder has written concerning his complete trust in God, "I would like to emphasize my way of life as a prisoner is no longer difficult."

However, forgiveness is a two-way street. If we ask it for ourselves, then we must accord it to others, regardless of the circumstances. We pray, "Forgive us as we forgive . . ." This phrase was embodied in the model prayer so that we would not only pray it but meditate on it every day. From first to last, forgiveness was high on the Master's priority list. Even on the cross he taught it. Still it is one of the most difficult lessons we have to learn.

Wherever there are people, there are differences, personality conflicts, resentment, and even bitterness. We are prone to argue that we are justified in feeling as we do, but with the coming of our Lord the law of an eye for an eye was abolished, and in its place was forgiveness. Vengeance is no longer ours. It is a responsibility we leave to God. To forgive is to forget, to start anew. Difficult, yes, but not impossible with his help and example. This is the only way to overcome evil and estrangement. It is the way of the cross.

Perhaps the transgression that causes one of the major problems and that we so easily overlook as we try to find time for quietness is the sin of busyness. We say we are busy doing for others. Jesus was also busy healing, teaching, and comforting, but he still took time to be with God.

Everyone of us needs time for daily meditation, the secret of power and union with God. This is where our Lord makes one of his great demands. He asks for our bodies, minds, and souls. We abandon self completely to him, trusting him to lead us and to direct our thinking and our actions. He asks no other help than our willingness. If we are willing, he is able. We may go to church, read the Bible, pray before retiring, return thanks at meals, and do for others, but spiritual growth remains impaired, even stunted, until we practice the presence of God as we would practice music, typing, golf, or any other activities that engage our attention.

There is a great lesson in Mark's Gospel. The disciples returned to Jesus and told him all they had done and taught; he replied, "Come away by yourselves to a lonely place, and rest a while" (Mark 6:31).

To be alone with God is the only way in which we will gain a true perspective of life as he would have us live it. During times of quietness we gain wisdom, vision, steadfastness, and the power to meet the unexpected.

While we are confessing our other transgressions and making the necessary corrections, it would be well to ask him to help us plan our activities so that we would have more time with him.

Contentment comes from within, not from without. When we are inwardly free, we have recovered our liberty. We are not just free of transgressions, but we are so free of self that we truly belong to God. Then, and not before, are we free of the anxieties, worries, and sorrows that belong to this earth and free of the everlasting drive to possess the things of the world.

Paul, who had made the transition, could write to his friends at Galatia, "But the fruit of the Spirit is love, joy, peace, patience, kindness, goodness, faithfulness, gentleness, self-control; against such there is no law" (Gal. 5:22–23).

10. A Star in the Sky

Often when I feel hemmed in by problems, I turn to my books or to music or art. Some people date a new era in their lives from reading a book or a poem or hearing a song that catches and holds them or from seeing a picture that conveys a great truth.

Instinctively, men and women are worshiping creatures, longing for ways to develop their innermost feelings and come into union with God.

Johnny Blenco, a character in Ernest Raymond's novel *The Mountain Farm*, says, "Just to trust that God is deep in one as the source of one's being can be a pretty happy business. To arrive at a final conviction must be, I suppose, a little less than infinite joy."

For those seeking to move into this realm, the fine arts offer many opportunities. Annually, at least, we turn back some twenty centuries to the heavenly host saying, "Glory to God in the highest, and on earth peace among men" (Luke 2:14).

That event has been the inspiration for the beautiful carols and meaningful hymns we sing at Christmas. Chants or songs have been used since the beginning of civilization. In King Solomon's temple were three thousand priests with harps, trumpets, and psalteries, and there were many singers.

The poet has said:

> God is its author, and not man: he laid
> The keynote of all harmonies; he planned
> All perfect combinations, he made
> Us so that we could hear and understand.

Evelyn Underhill has written, "Spiritual reading is, or at least it can be, second only to prayer as a developer and support of the inner life."

In *A Journey with the Saints* Thomas Kepler tells of a conversation with a friend who said: "Fifteen years ago I was teaching religion on an American college campus. I found myself in a state of religious perplexity. I seemed to be unhappy as I found my religious ideas shifting. At that time I began to read *The Imitation of Christ* each morning before I taught my classes. That book of devotional readings 'saved' me into a new enthusiasm for daily living. It helped me get along with myself."

In the main, the paths are already charted by those dedicated persons; yet each must find the way best suited to his or her individual needs and go on from there. Books of this kind are not to be skimmed or hurried through; they are to be read and ingested. For my book mark I keep a card on which I have copied these words of Thoreau: "The most useful possession a man can have is the determination not to be hurried."

Not to be hurried . . . How many times have I glanced at some great truth, then rushed on to something else, thinking that at a later date when I have more time I will come back, little realizing that we get so involved with the press of living that we have little time for life.

Admittedly I may wander far afield in some of my reading. I like to turn to "Sky Lines and Wood Smoke" by the late Badger Clark, at one time poet laureate of South Dakota:

God meets me in the mountains when I climb alone and high,
  Above the wrangling sinners and gangling devotees,
Up where the tapered spruce will guide my glances to the sky
  And canyon walls will mutely preach their mighty homilies
In hush so dense that I can sense—is it my pulses drumming?
  Or God's light footfall, coming through the silvery aspen
    trees?

In her book *Country Chronicle*, Gladys Taber has written: "There are so many silences—so many I would like to write a book about them, beginning with the first pulsing silence after the words 'I love you . . .' to the heavy quiet after a tragic piece of news.

"There is the stillness of a summer moon and the quiet of ebb tide. But I think perhaps the winter-morning stillness has the most magic. Quite literally there is no sound. And therefore the motionless air seems to sing—a melody from the beginning of time. I cannot analyze it, but my heart also stands still."

I thrill to Edwin Way Teale's books. He and his wife travel leisurely; they do not jam-pack miles into hours, and he writes about it so well. He makes one smell the new-mown hay, hear the mowing machine, see the field mice scamper ahead of the sickle. There is time to watch a meadowlark on a fence post or examine a rare fern. There is time to listen to the sound of the wind and the voices of those who lived close to the land.

With so much violence in our literature today it is refreshing to turn to Hal Borland, for he brings the New England countryside to our Southern apartment. At night, after a day battling city traffic, I walk out to stand with him in imagination and watch the stars, and a sense of peace comes over me.

My grandfather, who pioneered in Minnesota before it was a state, always went outside before going to bed to determine the next day's weather. Of course, with all the weathercasts on TV and radio that is no longer necessary; yet it is good to walk outside and in a moment of quietness see that all the stars are still in place and then say a trusting goodnight to the world.

Then there is Sigurd Olson. In his book *Open Horizons* he tells of a wilderness guide, Buck Sletton, who said, "Remember, no matter how cold and wet you are, you are always warm and dry."

To be cold and wet on the outside, yet to remain warm and dry—what a thought to live by.

Sometimes when I run into a bit of adversity, I turn to Olson's *Singing Wilderness* and the chapter "Scrub Oak." It is a beautiful description of scrub oaks' struggling for life on a rocky crag overlooking a northern lake where they are exposed to all the torments of that harsh climate. When I wrote to tell him how much I appreciated the chapter, he went out and picked three russet leaves in all their autumn glory and sent them to me. I have them before me now as I write, and for just a moment I am standing on that point, listening to the haunting cry of loons and looking to far off vistas.

Music! It cannot be defined. It is the marching song of saints, a beautiful summer night, and a breeze whispering a lullaby. Music is the distant peal of bells calling a weary world to rest and worship. It can only be listened to with the heart, and little by little it transports the soul to that place where inner voices are heard. It dispels sorrow, heals wounds, and quiets tumult. It speaks a language all its own that is universal for all who take time to listen and appreciate.

Of course, I have my favorites. I know how dangerous it is to mention favorites, for those that are meaningful to one may not bring a similar response from another. I so much like the Mormon Tabernacle Choir's "Come, Come Ye Saints." I picture courageous pioneers struggling against insurmountable obstacles. Because of their tremendous faith, they made the desert blossom like a rose.

Or again I may listen to Bill Mann sing "My Faith Looks Up to Thee" or "Fill My Cup." I need that kind of faith. I remember a thought from a meditation in Silent Unity's devotional guide, *Daily Word:* "God is the ocean and I am a drop. The substance of the drop is the same as the whole ocean."

There was a meeting of Methodist Men at Purdue University some years ago when Mr. Mann led five thousand men in that great hymn "How Great Thou Art." During that weekend, wherever men could find a piano, they sang that hymn until it literally became a part of the church. Of course, I know George Beverly Shea did much to bring it to prominence. Most of us had heard him sing it before we sang it at Purdue and were grateful to him for it.

Recently I was given the record "Peace and Joy and Power." Words and music come from the Christian Science hymnal with singer Larry Groce. The simple melody, the guitar, the wooden flute, and the harpsichord weave great thought patterns.

And what greater lift to one's faith than the words of the old preacher in "Alleluia, a Praise Gathering for Believers" when he says, "Fifty-four of my seventy years have been spent in the wonderful service of the Lord . . . At sixteen I committed my life to Christ and I've been serving him ever since. And that's why at seventy I have no complaints."

There are almost no limits to my favorites depending on my mood and the need—Mozart, Schubert, Faure, Quantz's Sonatas for Flute Ensembles, Grofé's "Grand Canyon Suite." I thrill especially to the last one. Somehow, in the music the composer has captured the spell of that geographical wonder, and for the moment I am transported to it and stand on the rim watching the changing colors, sensing the awe and majesty that hover over the area, even though I am hundreds of miles away.

There is also a time for Ferrante and Teicher, Mantovani, Glenn Miller, and Lawrence Welk.

Yes, I plead guilty to a growing appreciation for country and Western music. Sorrow, loneliness, the blues, love, and forgiveness are passions common to people the world over. But in the rural areas, in the wide open spaces, and in the mountains these raw emotions have found their way into music to express man's deeper feelings. They are simple, heart-felt longings and speak of God and creation in the same humble fashion they deal with all of life.

I love the spirituals, those great songs of the black people. Most are of a distinctly religious character. They embody a deep yearning to understand God and be reconciled to the burdens life entails.

Sometimes after listening to one of these records, I find a stillness in my soul that enables me to pray and listen with a new confidence and quietness.

What do I think about when the world fades away with its demands and its din? I have no planned pattern. I may not think at all. My mind may just float like a cork on a calm water; then suddenly an idea will germinate. It may be something I have done or need to do. It may be an idea for an article I am writing. It may be something far from the usual demands of life.

The Apostle Paul gave some sage advice when he wrote, "Whatever is true, whatever is honorable, whatever is just, whatever is pure, whatever is lovely, whatever is gracious, if there is any excellence, if there is anything worthy of praise, think about these things" (Phil. 4:8).

Tennyson expressed a similar idea: "Self-reverence, self-knowledge, self-control, these three alone lead to sovereign power."

In our everlasting hurry we have lost the ability to look inward, to be still, and to know that God is God. We cast aside ethics for the expediency of the moment. We have lost the true sense of values that can only come from the quiet heart where there is just God and the worshiper. "Acquaint now thyself with him, and be at peace" (Job 22:21, KJV).

This morning I could not seem to make my thoughts click, or at least I could not write what I was trying to say; so I put Ernest Bloch's *Sacred Service* (*Avodath Hakodesh*, or Morning Service) with Leonard Bernstein conducting the New York Philharmonic and Robert Merrill, cantor, on the stereo and listened to it in its entirety. I may have to work a bit later this evening, but it is worth that. This magnificent composition is rooted in the rich musical traditions of the Jewish people. I picture them across the centuries, laying the foundation stones for our Christian faith, and think how much we are indebted to them.

A quote from some forgotten source comes to mind: "May all created in thine image recognize that they are brethren, so that one in spirit and one in fellowship, they may be forever united before thee."

Just as truth and light are found in the satisfying world· of literature and music, they are also found in art.

Whenever I am in the nation's capital, if there are moments to spare, I go to the National Gallery of Art. The atmosphere of the place is one of quiet and rest. It is not a place where one hurries. Time stands still. Spectators move from room to room, even picture to picture, quietly and reverently.

It is always difficult for me to say which is my favorite in any art gallery because there are so many favorites just as in literature and music. Much depends on the mood, the need that one brings to the viewing.

Sallman's *Christ at Dawn* always touches me deeply. "And in the morning, a great while before day, he rose and went out to a lonely place, and there he prayed" (Mark 1:35).

The artist has captured the beauty, not only of the words in Mark's Gospel, but of the dawn mists rising from the Sea of Galilee and the deep tints of early morning reflected in the blue waters. Across the lake the city is sleeping; still Christ is watching over it, praying for it, concerned about it, wishing perhaps that somehow its people could understand his dreams and purposes for them.

Robert Ferruzzi's *A Modern Madonna*, sometimes called Madonna and Child, evokes deep memories. A beautiful young mother, perhaps on a busy city street or even a country road, still a bit awed by the responsibility that is hers, is thinking, "This is my child. I will be patient. I will do my best. No harm must come to this life that is a very part of my life." It is a mother's love, the most nearly perfect human love.

In Clemens von Zimmermann's *Christ and the Fishermen* we see the deep influence of Christ on ordinary men. Zimmermann, a nineteenth-century German historical painter, has captured the concern Christ feels and expressed it in the face of the aged father, Zebedee. While Zebedee wants to encourage his two sons to heed the call, deep down inside he is counting the cost, asking what it will mean. But the call of the Master is great; it will not be denied.

The Master's words, "If any man would come after me, let him deny himself and take up his cross and follow me" (Matt. 16:24), suddenly take on personal meaning.

Without too much imagination one can see both tragedy and trust in the face of Christ in Heinrich Hofmann's *Christ in Gethsemane*. Hofmann, another nineteenth-century German historical painter, is best known for a series of scenes from the life of Christ. In this one he portrays the loneliest spot in the loneliest of hours; yet the Master finds time to pray. He is not running madly around to hire lawyers to represent him at his coming trial, nor is he looking for an army of defenders with swords and spears. There is only one avenue—quiet, trusting, humble prayer. This painting says to me that at times everyone is absolutely alone with God and that none other is able or adequate.

In such moments we say, "Lord, I am yours—body, mind, and soul. I give myself to you without reservation." But it must be more than mere words soon forgotten. It must be total commitment.

At this point Hannah Whitall Smith in her book *The Christian's Secret of the Happy Life* has been of tremendous help to me. She has written: "It is a very simple transaction, and yet very real. The steps are but three: First we must be convinced that the scriptures teach this glorious indwelling of God; then we must surrender our whole selves to him and be possessed by him; and finally we must believe that he has taken possession, and is dwelling in us."

11. Arbors and Cathedrals

In her poem *Aurora Leigh*, Elizabeth Barrett Browning wrote, "Earth's crammed with heaven and every common bush afire with God."

Charles Hanson Towne, a twentieth-century American poet, said, "The hills are mute; yet how they speak of God."

The psalmist sang, "I lift up my eyes to the hills. From whence does my help come? My help comes from the Lord, who made heaven and earth" (Ps. 121:1–2).

At times we desire silence and solitude above all else. To let the wilderness or the mountains close in on all sides and shut out the noises of the world brings us into a sense of union with the Creator that is both beautiful and soul satisfying. To be out under the sky, to feel the earth, the sun, the wind, the flowers and trees, is to let God's creations work their magic in his greatest creation—the person.

Henry David Thoreau stated it well:

"I sat in my sunny doorway from sunrise till noon, rapt in a reverie, amidst the pines and hickories and sumacs, in undisturbed solitude and stillness, while the birds sang around or flitted noiselessly through the house, until the sun falling in my west window, or the noise of some traveler's wagon on the distant highway, I was reminded of the lapse of time. I grew in those seasons like corn in the night, and they were far better than any work of the hands would have been. They were not subtracted from my life, but so much over and above my usual allowance."

God has given us a beautiful universe, and a moment comes when it is necessary to let it into one's fibers to ease the tensions of the day. In nature there is a timeless swing, a ceaseless rhythm, that catches one up for the moment and shuts out the little human things. In the out-of-doors an undertone of life speaks of eternity, humbles, yet reaches into the deepest recesses of our being and touches the immortal flame. It confirms the words of the sage: "While earth remains, seedtime and harvest, cold and heat, summer and winter, day and night, shall not cease" (Gen. 8:22).

To look at a mountain, a giant redwood, the ocean, even a grain of sand, is to sense the presence of mighty forces beyond comprehension. There is a beauty, a majesty, that says, "Come and experience. Come and be at peace. Come and worship. Come and store up the memory of brooks and meadows, mountains and oceans, for those times when they are miles away yet can be experienced and help relax the tension caused by the demanding world."

I have been asked what in nature reminds me most of God. All of it, but most specifically blue violets in a woodsy glade, a spring bubbling from a hillside, the ethereal song of a white-throated sparrow, the fragrance of wild honeysuckle, the call of wild geese from a night sky, the scent of pine needles drying in the sun, a glacier-scarred rock, the surge of the tide, stars on a winter night. Only a loving God could have given us such beauty and wonder without clamor or fanfare. The marsh marigold does not announce its presence with a trumpet blast; the gemmed snowflake drifts gently to the ground; the grass makes no sound to proclaim that it is growing in obedience to the Creator's commands.

All my life I have appreciated those moments when I have been in the midst of God's manifestations of life; his unfailing laws proclaim creation and growth as well as age and transition. I praise him for being at work in my life to bring constant renewal and usefulness just as he does for all creation. While I sense God in the glory of the sunset, the beauty of a flower, the lilting song of a bird, I know this is only part of him.

Perhaps Tennyson was able to say it better than any other:

> Flower in the crannied wall,
> I pluck you out of the crannies,
> I hold you here, root and all, in my hand.
> Little flower—but *if* I could understand
> What you are, root and all, and all in all,
> I should know what God and man is.

In these times I know my greatest need is to come into union with God, let him flow through me and beyond me out into the world. While I have felt his presence in many places—the clamor of the newsroom, the bustle of the airport, the marketplace—I sense it in a wonderful way in the quietness of nature. To experience him in the silences of the soul is to give an added beauty to the sunrise, the flowers, the birds, the dew upon the grass. For a moment just to be away from noise, traffic, the shriek of sirens, the blare of radio and television, the power lawn mower, the insistent clamor of the telephone, and to be where there are no sounds but those that nature makes is a bit of heaven.

Perhaps that is why I like to walk out as night fades and have the dawn all to myself. I am alone in a world that has been refreshed with the cool stillness of the night. There is still a drowsy hush in the air; yet the first experimental notes of the birds proclaim that God is not only a creator but a renewer. I sense his life pulsating in the world and in me.

In the hush of the moment, whenever it be, I become quiet and fix my attention on some object or idea until I am still within, and gradually the beauty, the grandeur, and the joy predominate. The world with its cares fades, and prayer, not of words but a feeling of praise, develops, new ideas are born, sensitivity is intensified, more complete understanding emerges. There is a self-forgetting and an open receptivity to a greater good.

There was a time when life became almost too big to handle. I was resting beneath a couple of tall spruce while just above their tips a cap of clouds floated along in a midday sky that seemed to go on forever. On another occasion, from a mountaintop I watched the day fade from the sky and the deep purple of night fling its mantle over the wild and mysterious canyons. In both instances I felt a deep and profound quiet that stilled the tumult in my soul and became unbounded reverence.

When we turn to him in this fashion, he brings us into harmony with him and reveals his way. When we are surrounded by the revelations of nature, not only do our problems seem more manageable, but we realize we are more than mind and body: We are a spirit created in the image of God. If we let it, our spirit truly becomes his spirit, and we have an understanding, a wisdom, a confidence, that lifts us and sends us on to realize our greater potential.

Often the cares of the world, the problems of people,

divert our attention from the presence of God. When I am alone in big, wild, wonderful places, I say with the psalmist, "How lovely is thy dwelling place, O Lord of hosts! . . . Even the sparrow finds a home and the swallow a nest for herself" (Ps. 84:1, 3).

In those moments I realize all things were made by him and belong to him. I remember an autumn day deep in the woods when silences were so tremendous the falling of an acorn sounded like a thunderclap. I don't know how long a squirrel had been regarding me from his perch high in the branches of an oak before the slight movement of his tail caught my attention. I had paused to rest on the fallen trunk of what had once been a giant in the forest of giants and soothed by the stillness of the place had lost the world, lost myself.

I tried to recall the lines of a forgotten poem about listening for invisible things. Suddenly I knew that was exactly what I was doing. I was listening, not with any degree of concern, but with a deep contentment that could only come on such an elfin day. It was one of those rare moments I would carry with me through the long, busy months ahead. I think it was there I realized that times of meditative quietness—the silences—were not an escape from the world but preparation for it. I had neglected this item too long, and I resolved to do something about it. While there might be long intervals when I could not return to such a setting, there could be times of quietness even in the heart of a city or in a gathering of people.

On a summer evening in Tennessee I was speaking to a large group of men. A whippoorwill's throbbing call came floating in through an open window, and I said, "Do you mind if we pause for a moment and listen?" I saw the smiles on their faces, but the hush that came over us, broken only by the voice of the whippoorwill, was probably more eloquent than anything I might have said.

On a subzero day deep in the Alaskan wilderness, Rog Thompson and I stood at Portage Glacier, gazing at its vibrant tones of blue and green that seemed to merge into the cloudless sky. Our frozen sandwiches thawed by an open fire, and together we returned thanks for the beauty of God's earth. We knew that glaciers might pass away but never God's love.

Later in the day we stopped at a little church with its pump organ and wood stove, a building so small Rog said the preacher could raise his hand to pronounce the benediction and open the door all at the same time. Even the Alaska earthquake, that Good Friday evening in March 1964, didn't erase the lilt from Rog's voice or the smile from his face. Somehow with the demanding schedule of a preacher he always finds time for the more important things —quietness and others.

Some years later in a Philadelphia hotel we prayed for a loved one who was miles away and critically ill, and we remembered those other moments of quietness we had shared. They were a source of strength and comfort.

Just as I have found moments of quietness in the wilderness, so I have found them in sanctuaries of all denominations wherever I have been. Whenever I am in New York City, if in the vicinity, I go to beautiful St. Patrick's Cathedral. While I am not of that faith, I do not find it incongruous to kneel with other worshipers and in the hush of the holy place experience God's presence. The rush, the jostle, and the clamor of the great city are forgotten, and there is a renewing quietness for both body and soul.

There was that bitter winter morning on the Chicago Loop when I paused in Chicago Temple mostly to get warm. Seeing a man, his coat collar still turned up around his ears, attaché case beside him, kneeling at the altar, I felt the urge to join him. He didn't know me, and I didn't know him, nor did we exchange a word, but somehow I felt a bond that made my day go better for the time spent there. The heart of the spiritual life is in adoration and commitment. Where better than at the altar of a church?

Often in my own church I look at the altar and think of the great dramas of life which have taken place there— sweethearts have been united in marriage, babies have been dedicated, commitments to Christ have been made, earthly goodbyes have been spoken to departed loved ones. And then I listen for the voice that said, "Behold I stand at the door . . . I will come in" (Rev. 3:20).

Sometimes it takes real effort to clear the mind of clutter so that we can extend the invitation to him to come in and work his will with us. It is letting him do more for us than we can ever ask or expect. It is a time when we forget all side issues, all human-made differences, and think only of his presence.

> Have you listened to the church bells
>   with their early morning call,
>   floating far across the meadows,
>   dipping deep in forest glen?
> Have you listened to the church bells
>   in the smoky city pall,
>   seeping in through broken windows,
>   felt the invitation then?
> Have you listened to the church bells
>   when the night begins to fall,
>   felt the softness of the shadows,
>   paused to pray with other men?
> Have you listened to the church bells
>   heard the Master's gentle call,
>   and been lifted from the hollows
>   to the heights of life again?

Not all of us can go to the forests and mountains, perhaps not even to church; yet in a city apartment there is a time and a place. So I once wrote for another book: "The quest is in the heart of all pilgrims who seek life's deeper meanings. Some find them by the lonely sea or in a mountain glen. Others find them in a soaring plane or in a humble cell. I found them in the silences, a place where all can go, just sitting by a window tall and looking at the sky."

Gladys Taber says as long as you have a window, life is exciting.

Edward Steichen, the famous photographer, had traveled the world over in search of unusual pictures. Then late in life he concentrated only on photographing those things he could see from the windows of his home and took hundreds of beautiful pictures without once venturing away.

And so God reveals his life to us in a tree outside our window, in a dandelion growing up through a crack in the pavement, in a blade of grass, as much as he does in an Alaskan glacier.

In "Auguries of Innocence," William Blake wrote:

> To see a World in a grain of sand
> And a Heaven in a wild flower,
> Hold Infinity in the palm of your hand,
> And Eternity in an hour.

In our apartment I have my typewriter near a window where I can look up at the sky. I often recall the words of Washington Irving in *Rip Van Winkle:* "Every change of season, every change of weather, indeed, every hour of the day, produces some change in the magical hues and shapes of the mountains . . ." So it is with the sky; day or night it is a source of beauty and wonder. It is always changing. There is activity overhead, clouds forming and moving. Colors from the most vivid to the soft pastel, violence and serenity, make their imprint on that great canvas reaching from horizon to horizon or skyline to skyline.

"The heavens are telling the glory of God; . . . Without a sound or word, silent in the skies, their message reaches out to all the world" (Ps. 19:1, 3, LB).

When I look at the vastness of the sky, I am no longer bounded by time and space. Little details that looked so large disappear like the last traces of a thunderstorm riding away over the city. I have stayed for hours at my window, watching the changing colors, the multiplicity of patterns. Who can do justice to such a panorama—the dawns, the sunsets, the storms, the moonlight?

Often when I have worked late at night, I turn out the lights, draw back the drapes, and revel in the beauty of the night sky. I walk out under the stars and, breathing deeply, think, "Truly this is handiwork of God."

Just last right we had a sharp electrical storm soon after one o'clock. I watched the lightning fork across the sky and wondered who conceived the idea of an energy shortage. With all God's power available, man worries about his own puny power. Perhaps one day we will not only harness energy from the sun but that of lightning as well. But after I watched the storm for awhile, with the wind whipping the locust tree out in the yard, I decided to leave such weighty matters to the scientist and went to bed.

About three o'clock I awakened and again went to the window. The storm had disappeared, but it had left a few torn clouds trailing behind. The moon, in its fourth quarter, came slicing along like a canoe riding the whitecaps on a great expanse of open water, and I thought all that great beauty is going to waste while most folks are sleeping.

Of course, there are those languorous nights in the late summer, even in the heart of the city, when Rae and I walk out to listen to the vibrant notes of the katydids—a lullaby, it seems to us. These are nights of fulfillment and maturity. There is a wholeness in the air as we sense the earth around us and God's presence. There is the assurance that he has again provided beauty, abundance, life. It is all a part of his love. It says to us that we need not wait until later; it is now. We are part and parcel of his divine love. All we have to do is claim it to make it a part of our lives and let it overflow into the lives of others. We thank him for his goodness and with expectancy say, "Tomorrow."

As night follows day, so winter follows summer. It too has a beauty, a deep sense of rest, though I must admit I much prefer the warmer seasons.

Often, while we were living in the Black Hills, we would go out on a winter night. If there was a moon, the shadows on the snow were like etchings, and we would wonder about the various designs and wish we were artists so that we might capture some of their ethereal beauty.

Yet there comes a time, summer or winter, to go indoors, close the drapes, and remember there is one who keeps eternal vigilance while we sleep.

12. Skyways and Detours

One can be quiet . . .

A friend has told of being on a plane traveling from John F. Kennedy International Airport to Boston. As he listened to the conversation of the passengers, he heard them sharing common experiences. When the occasion presented itself, he asked the stewardess who the passengers were. She explained that most were commuters who work in Europe all week and come home to the United States for the weekend.

We are a mobile society. Miles are no longer barriers to our work, but they can become barriers to a happy home life and a stable religious life unless we give some serious thought and discipline to it.

In *The Practice of the Presence of God*, Brother Lawrence could say: "The time of action is not different from that of prayer. I enjoy God with as great tranquility in the hurry of my kitchen, where frequently people call upon me at the same time for different things, as if I were on my knees at the holy sacrament."

Being aware of the presence of God, meditating about him and his relationship to us, is not merely an intellectual effort to master certain ideas about him or to psyche ourselves up as a player may before a game. Rather it is looking for him in everything we say and do, seeking him in everything we touch or that touches us. It is realizing our total dependence on him, remembering that he has no boundaries, that distance cannot limit him because he is wherever we are. It is being with him in the kitchen, at school, on the plane, in the office, in the hotel, or on the golf course. It is reaching for him even while he is reaching for us in strange as well as familiar surroundings, in sickness and health, during the Saturday night party and the Sunday morning worship service.

At the height of the noonday rush in a crowded restaurant, a friend leaned across the table and said, "There's got to be more to life than what I am getting. At times I feel as if I am being drawn through a knothole and the knot shoved in after me. I never quite get my feet on the ground before there is change, reorganization. I'm making a fair salary. There's no trouble at home, but I'm reaching for something and never quite make it."

"Like what?" I asked.

"Like my dad," he said. "He was a carpenter. On Sunday, after church and dinner we'd sometimes drive around town where we lived or go out in the country. Dad would point to a house or barn and say, 'I built that. It's as sound as the day I drove the last nail.' I want what he had—faith as strong as the nails he drove."

"What about your own faith?" I asked.

He shook his head. "Dad had time."

"And you don't?"

"Not really. Or maybe I do and don't know where to start, where to get a handle."

"And you want someone to tell you?"

"I want you to tell me."

I asked, "Why me?"

He said, "Because you write about such things. You've been in the rat race longer than I have."

I quoted the words that begin this book: "Better is a handful of quietness than two hands full of toil and a striving after wind."

He said, "Say that again."

I did.

"Who was the philosopher?" he asked.

"Some forgotten preacher." Then I gave him the reference.

He said, "I'll bet my dad knew that one. At noon when he was on the job, he'd find a quiet place and read his Bible or just sit and think. It used to look pretty dull to me."

"Does it still look that way?" I asked.

"It looks like heaven."

In a couple weeks I again had lunch with my friend. He said, "You know, I've been thinking about what you told me, especially about the words of that long-ago preacher, about a handful of quietness. Just thinking about them makes a difference. Already I've made a couple of changes that give me more time, but it isn't easy."

Many times I've thought about those conversations in the crowded restaurant and the ones who commute to

Europe or across the continent and have tried to tie them
in with the attitude that Brother Lawrence developed. I am
sure many of us can say, "I wish I had what he had." Few,
perhaps none, of us do, but we can strive for it, and hope-
fully bit by bit we may become more consistently aware
of God's presence until even snatched moments are wonderful.

One evening we were racing after the setting sun, hurled
by four jet engines. In the galley the stewardesses were preparing the supper trays. A few passengers were reading.
Others were trying to sleep, but, for the most part, those
who could had their faces pressed to the windows to absorb
the spell of the moment. The setting sun blazed through the
cloud-banked horizon, spraying it with savage reds and
golds, turning it all into a flaming glory. We were high, and
the jets were driving us higher to carry us above the up-
thrust Rockies. Somewhere below were towns and ranches
with people going about their normal affairs, preparing the
evening meal, going home from stores and offices, working
in barns, perhaps getting ready for a party, absorbed in
their individual lives.

High in the sky our names and problems were as mean-
ingless to them as theirs were to us, playing hopscotch with
mountains and plains many of them would never see. For
a moment it seemed terribly dramatic that we could be
there so detached from the world and yet a part of it. It
was one of those moments of awe and wonder, impossible
to convey to another, a moment of indescribable beauty,
a fleeting second before the darkness ringed us in; yet not
one of us was hidden from the eye of one who knows even
when a sparrow falls. With those thoughts I gave thanks
for the food that was placed before me, prepared by one
who perhaps was already home sitting in front of TV
watching the evening news. How far apart, yet closely
linked by an invisible bond of love to the Creator who had

breathed life into each of us and who would chart a course for us, even as the pilot was charting the course of the plane.

In those moments I knew a peace, a calm, a joy, that was as wonderful as the sunset. The days of preparation for the trip, the hurried finish of a manuscript, the last-minute letters to be dictated, and the dash to the airport were as far in the past as if it had all been dated B.C. And the future . . . as yet it had not arrived, and so for the moment, all any of us have, I felt a deep contentment.

When supper was finished and my tray taken up by the stewardess, I switched off my light and returned to the window. Night had drawn a curtain over the earth, but overhead the stars were beginning to wink on in the soft velvet sky. I have flown often on moonlit nights, but that moonless night had a beauty all its own. I think I felt as close to the Creator as I have ever felt, not because we were five miles up, but because for the first time in several days I was experiencing a happy calm, an inner security that was all too rare.

I knew by the stars that we were swinging north and west in a great arc and thought this is a moment I must remember. Sometimes when life gets all jammed up, I will take it out of the deep recesses of my mind and enjoy it all over again. Perhaps the memory of it will still whatever is tearing at me, pressing me to drive ahead, and I will know the present is all I ever have; so I will hang on to it with peace and joy.

Again and again, even in the life of the busiest, moments come to us as a gift from God if we recognize them.

That March evening the blizzard was already churning the Dakota prairies when the train left Minneapolis. In the shelter of the city there was only a slow wind, but as the train angled toward the Dakotas, the force of it picked up and the stars dimmed out. I went to bed and was sleeping soundly when we left Minnesota behind and crossed into North Dakota. It was one of a multitude of nights that I slept on a train, and I did not feel it stop. When I awakened in the darkness, there was a different motion as the car rocked beneath the full fury of the storm slamming against it, covering and chilling it with a mantle of driven snow.

It was to be some fifty hours before we were finally released from those drifts that paralyzed the upper Midwest for nearly a week. The train was finally uncoupled so the coaches and pullmans could be taken back to a small town where heat could be piped in and where food was available for the more than two hundred persons whose journeys were interrupted. At first there were moments of concern and a bit of irritability, but when the magnitude of the storm was apparent, it became a wonderful occasion. People, at a time such as that, are at their best. We shared. We visited. We cared for one another.

And there were those moments of quietness, even with the demon shriek of the wind filling every crack and crannie, to think of one who could say, "Peace be still," and the tempest stilled.

There was that time when the bus I took from San Francisco to Stockton was scheduled to reach its destination so that I might fill a noon luncheon speaking engagement, but before we had gone too many miles, it was evident there were some mechanical difficulties. Until then I had been absorbed in watching the landscape, but as the difficulties increased, I realized I had one thing very much in common with a Catholic priest sitting across the aisle from me: We were both looking at our watches with increasing concern. Until then we had not spoken to each other, but after a lengthy delay he said, "I have a noon speaking engagement. Right now it doesn't look as if I will make it."

I replied that I was in a similar situation.

After a few casual remarks he said, "I guess there isn't much we can do about it; so we might as well relax." He took a small book from his pocket and began to read.

As I watched him I thought of the description Willa Cather had written of Father Latour in *Death Comes for the Archbishop:* "The traveller dismounted, drew from his pocket a much worn book, and baring his head, knelt at the foot of the cruciform tree . . . Everything showed him to be a man of gentle birth—brave, sensitive, courteous. His manners, even when he was alone in the desert, were distinguished. He had a kind of courtesy toward himself, toward his beasts, toward the juniper tree before which he knelt, and the God whom he was addressing."

When my neighbor across the aisle had finished reading, he said, "This is wonderful. It is in English now although it used to be in Latin." He held the book to me.

In a matter of moments we were in deep conversation. Finally he said, "I have a difficult schedule ahead. Will you pray for me?"

A bit surprised I said, "You, a Catholic priest, are asking a Protestant layman to pray for you?"

He said, "I would appreciate it if you would."

There in the bus we had a few moments of silent prayer and then promised to remember each other that way during the days ahead.

Fortunately, the difficulty the bus was having was corrected, and we both made our engagements with moments to spare, but in that time together a friendship was born. Because of the interest I expressed in the material he was using, he sent me the devotions he used every evening and suggested that perhaps my wife and I would like to use them together. And so we did.

While we did not pray in exactly the same manner he did, it was both a humbling and warming experience to know that for at least a few minutes each day we were sharing with a Jesuit priest, though miles apart, in adoration of the God we all served.

There was that time when the band around my chest was getting tighter and tighter. No pain, just a tightness that would not go away.

The verdict—cancel all engagements for six months. Engagements had been scheduled for as much as a year in advance; trips had been anticipated; work was waiting. After the first moments of disappointment, wonderful days and weeks became time to be quiet and think. There was time to write a book that perhaps would never have been written under normal conditions. That has brought a real sense of accomplishment, especially with schedules once again filled.

And then there were the astronauts speeding toward the moon, taking time to read, "In the beginning God . . ."

Yet it is not only in the beginning. For Brother Lawrence it was all the time, even in the kitchen.

Perhaps more than anything we need to arrive at a balance, at a discipline of work, play, love, and worship that will be more than mere living. It will be life itself. At the center of these four disciplines, worship is the key. In worship we try to determine how best we can intermingle work, play, and love, yet place ourselves in such a receptive mood that God's energy, wisdom, and love can supplement our human frailty.

13. Blazed Trails

The goal of those who would snatch moments of quietness for union with God is not merely to rest in a time of happy sensation. More nearly those are the times a mountaineer takes to build up his resources while pausing on a ledge before going on to the summit.

The names of those who have blazed this trail for others to follow are legion.

Often in my quiet times I find myself thinking about Mohandas Gandhi, not a Christian in the literal sense of the word, yet one who embodied in his daily life many principles taught by our Lord. Never do I think about him but I recall the words of Zechariah: "Not by might, nor by power, but by my Spirit, says the Lord of hosts" (Zech. 4:6).

For ninety years (1858–1947) India was ruled directly by Great Britain. However, in 1920, Gandhi, a Hindu, issued his call for a mass movement of nonviolence and non-cooperation, a move that was to take more than a quarter-century to achieve its goal. At no time did the Mahatma have wealth or an army at his disposal, nor was he a great organizer, but he was a superb leader.

Historians attribute Gandhi's success as a leader of the Indian people to four qualities: truth, compassion, courage, and simplicity. While many persons have some of these traits as part of their lives, Gandhi made them his life without equivocation.

He equated truth with God. He did not merely think it or teach it; he lived it. He sincerely believed that one person and truth comprise a majority. As a result he was free to face anyone, even the might of the British Empire, because never once did he depart from this belief for the sake of expediency.

To tell an untruth, regardless of its purpose, was for him unthinkable. Once when told that truth had no place in politics, he quickly differed with the speaker. To resort to such tactics was a sign of laziness and weakness, he insisted.

We might hold up our lives to this standard for careful scrutiny. Can we live by such a demanding code? It would tax anyone to say the least—a little white lie now and then to ease the way . . . But would it lead to freedom to talk it over with God, to face others without hesitation or cover-up?

Compassion was another of Gandhi's hallmarks. He once remarked that his ambition was to wipe every tear from every eye. In that respect he was more than a politician making a speech for reelection, more than an idle dreamer hoping for a utopia sometime, somewhere. He was speaking from the heart of a person to persons who knew and under-stood the bitterest of suffering, the depths of sorrow, the sting of failure. Compassion was a great word as he used it.

I think for a moment . . . that sales person today . . . was she hurting? She didn't say so, but it was written in every line of her face. For only a moment she sat down, then as quickly jumped up. She forced a smile to her lips, but her eyes showed suffering. How many eyes show suffering? Gandhi wanted to wipe every tear from every eye. He understood because he had suffered.

Courage! Never once did Gandhi falter. He could and did endure prison, physical and mental suffering. Often he faced death for his convictions; yet he had a song on his lips. On one occasion he remarked, "My ambition is to change the British people through nonviolence and make them realize the harm they have done to India. I do not want to harm them. I want to serve them as I serve my own."

Recently I was talking with a peace officer. He said, "I have worn a gun and badge for twenty-two years, but I have never drawn my gun against any person. I hope I never need to."

He had been on duty during racial violence. He had been called names. He had taken abuse, but he embodied compassion and courage.

Perhaps Gandhi was best known for his simplicity. Few remember that in his youth he dressed in the highest fashion of his day. Instead, they remember him as a half-naked individual with a sheetlike robe draped over one shoulder and a pair of scuffed sandals. In that garb he became a symbol of India's poverty so that all the world might see. He became one of the masses. He dressed, ate, and lived exactly as they did. They could come to him with their hurts without waiting outside paneled doors.

Knowing that the majority of his people had to work at the most menial tasks, he too worked at least one hour each day at his spinning wheel and insisted that all true followers of his do the same. There was dignity and independence, he believed, even in the humblest of tasks.

Quite often after thinking about Mohandas Gandhi, I turn to a piece written by William Henry Channing: "To live content with small means; to seek elegance rather than luxury; and refinement rather than fashion; to be worthy, not respectable; and wealthy, not rich, to study hard, think quickly, talk gently, act frankly; to listen to stars and birds, to babes and sages, with open heart; to bear all cheerfully, do all bravely, await occasion, hurry never, in a word, to let the spiritual, unbidden and unconscious grow up through the common. This is to be my symphony."

When I meditate on that awhile, I think I would stack it up with the best music. If more people would follow those sage words, we'd have happier, more contented people, fewer broken homes, and a big drop in our crime rate.

While I have been writing these pages, word has come of a long-time friend, a college roommate, who has just retired after forty years of teaching, thirty-six of them in the same public school system where he was the high-school speech teacher and dramatic coach. Some things said about him at his retirement dinner, and that I have known about him, seem to fit into what I am trying to write.

I once asked him what he did when students in his class were frightened over making a speech. He replied, "The first day or two I always manage to have the class laugh at me a few times. Then we have some days when everyone gets laughed at. Once folks find it doesn't hurt to be laughed at and they get to where they can laugh at themselves, there is no longer any problem."

That he has been successful when others have become discouraged and dropped by the wayside is attested to by the fact that a new high-school auditorium has been named for him. In making the announcement the superintendent said, "Awards such as this do not happen to common people because common people do ordinary things. The naming of this school facility for a man can only happen to an uncommon man, because an uncommon man does extraordinary things. This man has been an uncommon teacher because he always had extra time to do things for his students."

I remember stopping for coffee in the little Minnesota town where he taught so long. I asked the waitress if she knew a Mr. Martin. With a voice akin to reverence she said, "You mean Charley Martin? I took every course he taught."

One of his supervisors said, "He was the type of man who brought self-esteem, self-confidence, and desire to his students, who could inspire and motivate them, both in and out of the classroom. He enhanced the quality of life for many, many students, and he did so with humor."

As a father and grandfather he has carried these same high qualities into his home. Would that the world had more such uncommon men and women who would give their lives to such a demanding profession, rear a family of quality in these changing times, take their places regularly in church and in community affairs as he has done. He has embodied all the characteristics about which William Henry Channing wrote.

Whenever I think about some of the great folks the world has known, I am reminded of these words: "Since we are surrounded by so great a cloud of witnesses, let us also lay aside every weight, and sin which clings so closely, and let us run with perseverance the race that is set before us" (Heb. 12:1).

Perhaps in this day when so many old landmarks are fast disappearing we need to write four words on the tablets of our memory: *truth, compassion, courage, simplicity.*

14. Deeper than Deep

Four of us were having breakfast together—Wanda and Roy Borgstadt, Rae and I. They were driving through Nashville and naturally called us. Thirty years before we had been stationed at air bases in Illinois and Nebraska. At one time we had lived in the same duplex, they downstairs and we upstairs. Those were years when one made close friendships and stood shoulder to shoulder because there was no notion as to what the next hour might bring. Of course, we kept in touch by letters at Christmas and a few other special occasions. During the intervening years we had become parents and grandparents, but we took up right where we left off. In the course of our conversation Roy said, "We have been fortunate. We have had good marriages."

Since that morning I have thought often of our conversation and have asked, What makes a good marriage?

Naturally there is love in a good marriage, but we have become so mixed up in our thinking about love—*eros, agape*, romantic—that nobody knows for sure what is meant by the word.

I am sure that when two people fall in love there is physical attraction, call it what you will. But if a marriage is to endure and ripen into a relationship in which there is communication even though words are not spoken, there must be something more. So I would place friendship high on the list. A husband and wife must be friends, knowing the best and the worst, sharing common interests big and little, talking, laughing, crying, and enjoying together.

That calls for understanding, a give-and-take in which each tries to outgive the other, putting the other first. In the Garden of Eden the command was given, "Therefore a man leaves his father and his mother and cleaves to his wife, and they become one flesh" (Gen. 2:24).

To be one, there must be trust. When a husband or wife says of the other, "I know I can trust him or her regardless of the circumstances," another tie has been cemented. Trust in the highest sense of the word is more than mere faithfulness to the marriage vows. It also includes dependence, leaning on the other for strength and comfort.

During a lunch period a friend blurted out, "If I could only talk with my wife. My job is driving me up the wall, but I have no one to talk with. I go home at night, not knowing which way to turn, but my wife is so engrossed in her interests she hasn't time to listen, and if she did, she would probably say, 'That's your problem.' "

Midway through the seventeenth century Jeremy Taylor, English clergyman and writer, said, "Marriage is a school of exercise of virtue . . . marriage is the nursery of heaven . . . it hath in it less of beauty, but more of safety, than the single life; it hath more care, but less danger; it is more merry, and more sad; it is fuller of sorrows, and fuller of joys; it lies under more burdens, but is supported by all the strengths of love and charity, and those burdens are delightful."

Presently there is about one divorce for every three marriages; perhaps in our quiet times it would be well to give more attention to marriage, to its vows and what they truly mean. If homes decay, a nation decays.

The law of love works whether it be in marriage, between parents and children, friends, business associates, even countries, but we have to work at it continuously and in complete faith that together we can solve problems and experience life at its best. No person can adequately live alone. Try to separate ourselves as we will, we cannot. Like the warp and woof of a rug, our lives are woven together by innumerable, intricate relationships. The man or the woman on skid row, the convict, the angry militant carrying a banner or placard, the love-starved child, the lonely old man, the patient with a terminal illness, the clean, the well-housed, and the completely adjusted are all a part of our lives and we cannot shut them out. They too are children of God, and having one Father makes us brothers and sisters.

Love! What a tremendous word. How many persons critically ill, given up by doctors, have been brought back to health by the love of parents, children, a husband or wife, a love that supplies unfathomable strength? The number would be astonishing if such a record were available. How many persons whose lives have been marred by complete failure, crime, attempted suicide, have literally been loved back to victory and accomplishment? Only God knows. Where there is great love, there are great miracles. Never underrate the power of love.

But where does love begin? Perhaps with self, for unless self has value, meaning, respect, there is little basis for reaching out to others and finally to God where there is reciprocal action.

Always the world has desperately needed the love of God. Compassion is the life of God at work in the world. It is translated through each group or individual who is sensitive to the needs of others and reaches out with the healing touch. The greatest translation of the Scriptures is the way we live them. Nothing short of that can bind up the wounds of the world. If we are to experience true union with God, we must have meaningful relationships with one another.

Today the nations of the world are forming into two armed camps, each striving to outrace the other in producing destructive weapons. Distrust, suspicion, misunderstanding, and broken agreements are everywhere. Individuals, as well as nations, are struggling in the midst of a complex world of fast-moving change to find meaning and relationship. If only we could remember that the greatest safeguard against evil is love! War and violence are human-made monsters to satisfy lust and greed that begin with the individual.

A woman said, "I am a complete failure. I never achieved one single goal I had as a girl."

I asked, "Is there anyone you love, or who loves you?"
"Why of course." She seemed surprised at my question.
"Then you are not a failure. If you can be a success at just one thing, love, then you are not a failure."

Perhaps I was remembering Robert Louis Stevenson, who said: "So long as we love, we serve; so long as we are loved by others, I would almost say that we are indispensable; and no man is useless while he has a friend."

Or it could have been the old monk in Dostoevski's

Brothers Karamazov who advised his followers: "Love all God's creation, the whole and every grain of sand in it. Love every leaf, every ray of God's light. Love the animals, love the plants, love everything. If you love everything you will perceive the divine mystery in things."

If we ever feel unwanted, unloved, it is time to pause and realize that we are important to God, that he had a purpose for us from the time of creation—to be channels through which he could express his love. Just as we are incomplete without God, he is incomplete without us. If for the moment we doubt that, simply ask, Why did God create human beings? As we try, in our niche, to express his love, we will find his purpose for us becomes increasingly clear. We are beloved children of the Creator-God. He has endowed us with spiritual power to love and be loved. Rich or poor, regardless of color or looks, his love is in us to direct and lead us along a path of divine order. He is our source of love, power, and supply. Our good is his greatest wish.

Although living in harmony with others can be demanding at times, there is a way to release each person to the Creator, the Father of us all. There is a way to release rather than to judge or condemn, and no matter how much we may disapprove of his or her action, we hide that disapproval with love. If we cannot do that, at least we do not judge.

A man came to me at a retreat where I was speaking and said, "You can talk all you want about love and understanding, but there is one person I hate, and I can't help it."

I asked, "Have you ever tried praying for that person?"

He said, "I wouldn't be honest if I did."

I replied, "Well, at least pray that he gets what you think he has coming to him!"

He looked at me in disbelief. "I couldn't do that. Why . . . Why . . ." He smiled, "I see what you mean."

Each day, perhaps several times each day, we need to pray "Our Father . . ." until automatically when we meet another or have business dealings, even when we play together, we think "Our Father." This removes barriers. It brings us together in his love that is all encompassing.

As we ask God to bless all persons, even those we may dislike, freedom comes because when we set others free we too are free from one of the most destructive emotions known to humankind. When we hate another, we bind ourselves to that one through our hatred, an emotion that will warp and eventually destroy us if left uncontrolled. When we cease to dictate, when we stop judging, when we quit making decisions for another and put a brake on ourselves, harmony is restored.

Much friction in the world today is a result of our trying to be in control. Often we think in terms of big I and little you. This is not love; it is ego, self. When love is lacking, mistakes are made, tensions build, life is disturbed. Hate and distrust are negative forces. Love is the positive force that builds and cements together.

Often we say, "As I have come to know him or her for what he or she is really like, I have had a feeling of respect, even love." When we come to know, it makes a difference.

To learn to love is the supreme challenge. The greater the challenge, the more we grow. Love comes from the heart and is steadfast, unchangeable. It endures the tests of time.

Vern and Edna Watkins, friends of over forty years, have had what Roy called a good marriage. Together we have all known depression, war, and parenthood. Time and distances have often separated us for long intervals; yet in a real sense we have come to depend on one another and to share in a wonderful way. Once Edna said, "No matter what life dealt us, how deep the hurt, we would feel free

to come to you and know that you folks would understand." We have long considered that the supreme compli-
ment, the true meaning of friendship.

There is a solid happiness in having such friends. Time
and distance mean little. It is good to think about and
remember. Great as human love is, there is even a greater
love—divine love, God's love for us, our love for him.

Jesus came to earth in person so that we might better
realize and understand God's love. It was the greatest
demonstration of love ever given, but never think for a
moment that his love has left us. It lingers and grows in
the presence within.

In *The Sign of Jonas* Thomas Merton wrote, "He who
loves God is playing on the doorstep of eternity."

The heart of the teaching of Christianity is that it is not
we who have loved God but that he first loved us. St. John
of the Cross wrote, "God sustains and dwells in it sub-
stantially, even though it may be the greatest sinner in the
world. This union between God and creature always ex-
ists."

I often ponder those words when I hear our good friend
Stuart Joransen sing Lehman's "The Love of God." Stuart
has a beautiful, rich baritone voice, but when he sings that
great song it has a special meaning because I know he so
deeply believes the words he is singing. Many years ago
when I was trying to make a decision, we knelt at the altar
of the church where he was our pastor, and together we
prayed, each in his own way, silently. Those prayers,
perhaps as much as anything, brought about a decisive
change in my life, one I have never regretted.

Just as I believe in prayer, I sincerely believe the supreme
law of God is the law of love. In turn, he asks that we be
loving—that we love and accept his love and the love of
others. Through Christ, God's love went to the cross. Per-

haps our cross may be to love the unlovely, to be attentive to the cry of the least, to give up authority, prestige, and comfort, and to give our love as freely as he gave his.

Abu Yazid, the Moslem mystic, said, "I sought for God for thirty years; I thought it was I who desired him, but no, it was he who desired me."

In the twelfth century St. Bernard of Clairvaux said, "When God loves, he wants nothing else than to be loved; for he loves for no other purpose than that he may be loved, knowing that those who love him are blessed by that very love."

15. An Open Door

Much has been said about using the picture method, especially to remain calm, ready to deal with whatever life may throw at us. But there comes a time to create an even more important picture than calmness; it is when we stand in front of a mirror, look self in the eye, and ask, What kind of person do I wish to become?

Our Lord said, "Behold, I have set before you an open door" (Rev. 3:8).

This is a tremendous invitation; the door to becoming has been left wide open. To use that door is both a privilege and an opportunity. We need not go elsewhere to become someone we want to be. We can become that someone right where we are. Not only is there an opportunity to become, but there is an opportunity and responsibility to reach out to others.

A woman once said to a man, "You are a beautiful person both inside and out." In reality he was not that kind of person at all; yet her statement gave him an idea of what he might become—someone far better than he was. Bit by bit and prayer by prayer, he began to work at it. He had a picture of the person he could become, and he kept it ever before him until her statement became a living reality. This moment say, "I am a beautiful person, both inside and out." Then turn to God and affirm, "With your help I will."

Many times we are awed by the greatness of God, by his power and majesty; seldom do we realize that as individuals we have been given the right to claim that we are sons and daughters of his. We have been created in his image, in his likeness. What we may become is limited only by the extent of our imagination, our faith in him. In his Letter to the Ephesians, Paul said, "Now to him who by the power at work within us is able to do far more abundantly than all we ask or think" (Eph. 3:20).

We are still only scratching the surface of what we may become. Tens of thousands of persons are plodding along in mediocre roles. They "say" their prayers, attend church, have a quiet time, fling themselves frantically into good works, and accept the fact of God, but somehow they have never quite struck the fire of divine presence within. Our faith is often like a buried treasure, so close, yet of no use to us or anyone else.

I would venture to say that the majority of professing Christians are not totally committed to Jesus Christ. Oh, in a moment of high resolve we may make a commitment only to forget it quickly and go off willy-nilly to follow the caprices of our own desires or the call of the world, thereby missing out on the best our Lord has to offer. Only when we are totally committed to him and entirely obedient to his leading can he "tell you [us] great and hidden things which you [we] have not known" (Jer. 33:3).

In light of that, perhaps the earlier question should be reworded: What kind of person does the Lord want me to become?

To become the kind of person our Lord has in mind may well create a picture far different from the one we had for self. Most of us are willing to follow him part way but not all the way. We are not willing to place him above personal ambition and desire. We are not ready to commit our lives with unreserved obedience and follow his faintest suggestion without reservation. But when we do, when he is in complete control, miracles take place, forces are released, life is changed and supercharged. The glory of God in every person suddenly shines through when we get self out of the way and give it to him. Strangely enough, he does not take anything away except the clutter, smudges, and grime. He wipes life clean of these and gives it back much better than it has ever been or than we can make it by ourself.

Self is still there, but it has been transformed. An earthen vessel, it now radiates our union with God, not in pious words, but in dynamic living.

Personal ambition, recognition, prestige, and wealth may have been our main ambition. How small and trifling they become when we look at the true possibilities! Certainly we cannot escape the world; nor do we want to. We may suddenly find ourselves more involved in the world than ever before. On everyone who accepts Christ is placed the burden of living in the world and making a contribution to it. The bread and wine, the basin and the towel, must be so interwoven that work and worship, receiving and giving, quietness and action, are integral parts of the good life. While we are very much involved in the world, we must never get far from a constant awareness of God's presence in our lives—his power, love, and mercy. Just as we expect much from him, he expects from us. We ask him for courage, wisdom, direction, and health. He asks us for love, obedience, faith, and service. The door that is wide open is the door to Jesus Christ himself. Our Lord said, "I am the door" (John 10:7).

Often our religion has become *about* Jesus and not *of* Jesus; thereby its true meaning has been lost for many.

Jesus said, "I and the Father are one" (John 10:30).

From the beginning our goal has been a sense of union with God. This is where imagination, even mysticism, is necessary. What is mysticism? A depth of spiritual faith, the acceptance by faith of truths we cannot understand with the mind. Jesus accepted and lived by many truths even his disciples could not understand; as a result, they experienced miracles almost daily.

Evelyn Underhill has said, "Mysticism, however, is not an oddity or a mystery, but a term in religion which indicates that man has a warm and immediate feeling of God's spirit. It means that as a person breathes air into his lungs, so also a person breathes the spirit of God into his spirit. Mysticism believes that while the study of God is important, the test of our study is, do we experience God in our lives."

But how? how? how? The cry goes up on all sides.

Perhaps the first step is desire. Do I want to belong to God, body and soul, to be one with him even as Jesus was?

From time to time most of us have experienced this desire, but double-mindedness, our desire to have our cake and eat it too, has ruined our spiritual life. Even though we give intellectual assent to the fact that God is life, love, and intelligence, that he is omnipotent, omniscient, omnipresent, we are not quite ready to live by these facts. The transition usually does not come all at once. The external, the outer person, has assumed control too long. Perhaps we must follow the example of the prodigal son who decided, "I will arise and go to my father, and I will say to him, 'Father, I have sinned against heaven and before you'" (Luke 15:18). We do not blame others for our faults. We accept full responsibility. A man in his late eighties said, "God has been very good to me. Any mistakes I have made have been my own."

Having confessed, our next step is obedience. This calls for discipline. By effort we will turn our thoughts from the external and look to the inner, the real self, the spirit of God which is in us. In place of hate, resentment, bitterness, revenge, impurity, envy, jealousy, sickness, poverty, and all the many other imperfections, we begin to think thoughts of love, peace, trust, health, prosperity, and service. In times of quietness we think more and more in this realm until they become uppermost in our minds and actions.

No longer do we see self in the glass mirror; rather we see self in God's mirror—his written and spoken word. The eye of the soul becomes the eye with which we see. Our true conscience becomes our guide. That still small voice is not a human voice; it is the voice of our divine Creator. If thoughts or actions need to be eliminated from our lives, we eliminate them. Little by little there is a growing desire to bring the whole of life into conformity with the inner presence. As we realize our union with God, we no longer try to possess him; our desire is that he possess us. We have reached that decisive moment; we have decided for him. We are done with the old way. We begin the new. We have procrastinated long enough. We have made the decision to keep his commands, to accept his love, and to give him our love and deeds during our waking moments. The words of the prophet Micah give direction: "He has showed you, O man, what is good; and what does the Lord require of you but to do justice, and to love kindness, and to walk humbly with your God?" (Mic. 6:8).

It is a long, ardous journey but a thrilling one as we move to the great step in our times of quietness—humble adoration. On this subject Evelyn Underhill has written: "I am certain that we gradually and imperceptibly learn more about our God by this persistent attitude of humble adoration than we can hope to do by any amount of exploration. Adoration, as it more deeply possesses us, inevitably leads on to self-offering; for every advance in prayer is an advance in love."

In such times we discover we are praying without words, but words are not important. We are absorbed to the point where there is union, an expression of the soul . . . the sense of the presence of the one who not only put the stars in place but was before the universe existed.

We place ourselves in the hands of one who loves us far more than we can love ourselves, who thinks of our greatest good. Our hearts are filled with love and peace, and we become what it is we have in us to be—true children of God whose kingdom has always been where he rules the lives and hearts of men.

We can say with Paul, "For all the promises of God find their Yes in him. That is why we utter the Amen through him, to the glory of God" (2 Cor. 1:20).